DISCOVERING GENRE:

Poetry

Edited by

PAUL D. MOLIKEN

PRESTWICK HOUSE, INC.

"Everything for the English Classroom!"

P.O. BOX 658 CLAYTON, DELAWARE 19938

EDITOR: Paul D. Moliken

COVER AND TEXT DESIGN: Larry Knox

PRODUCTION AND LAYOUT: Jerry Clark

PRESTWICK HOUSE, INC.

P.O. BOX 658 • CLAYTON, DELAWARE 19938

TEL: 1.800.932.4593

FAX: 1.888.718.9333

WEB: www.prestwickhouse.com

Various and different versions of some of these poems do exist—Dickinson's
"Because I could not stop for Death" and Whitman's "Beat! Beat! Drums," for
example. In some cases, the differences are minor, a word or two; in other poems,
however entire stanzas are different. In deciding which version to print, Prestwick
House generally chose the one that was most commonly discussed in literary and
critical analysis.

ISBN-10   1-58049-315-7
ISBN-13 978-1-58049-315-4

DISCOVERING GENRE:

Poetry

CONTENTS

The Natural World

Technology and City Life

Society

Politics and Struggle

War

Religion

Emotion

Family

Love

Self-Knowledge

Death and Loss

A C K N O W L E D G M E N T S

•"Not Waving But Drowning" By Stevie Smith, from COLLECTED POEMS OF STEVIE SMITH, copyright ©1972 by Stevie Smith. Reprinted by permission of New Directions Publishing Corp.

•All lines from "Morning Song" from ARIEL by SYLVIA PLATH. Copyright ©1961 by Ted Hughes. Reprinted by permission of HarperCollins Publishers. For additional territory contact: The David Black Literary Agency, Inc., 156 Fifth Avenue, New York, NY 10011 Attn: Laureen Rowland.

•"Keeping Things Whole," from SELECTED POEMS by Mark Strand, copyright ©1979, 1980 by Mark Strand. Used by permission of Alfred A. Knopf, a division of Random House, Inc.

•"The Bean Eaters" By Gwendolyn Brooks. Reprinted by Consent of Brooks Permissions.

•"The Negro Speaks of Rivers" from THE COLLECTED POEMS OF LANGSTON HUGHES by Langston Hughes, copyright ©1994 by The Estate of Langston Hughes. Used by permission of Alfred A. Knopf, a division of Random House, Inc.

•"I Go Back to May 1937" from THE GOLD CELL by Sharon Olds, copyright © 1987 by Sharon Olds. Used by permission of Alfred A. Knopf, a division of Random House, Inc.

•"Those Winter Sundays." Copyright © 1966 by Robert Hayden, from COLLECTED POEMS OF ROBERT HAYDEN by Robert Hayden, edited by Frederick Glaysher. Used by permission of Liveright Publishing Corporation.

•Yusef Komunyakaa, "My Father's Love Letters" from Pleasure Dome: New and Collected Poems ©2001 by Yusef Komunyakaa and reprinted by permission of Wesleyan University Press.

•"My Papa's Waltz," copyright 1942 by Hearst Magazines, Inc., from THE COLLECTED POEMS OF THEODORE ROETHKE by Theodore Roethke. Used by permission of Doubleday, a division of Random House, Inc.

•"Her Lips are Copper Wire", from CANE by Jean Toomer. Copyright 1923 by Boni & Liveright, renewed 1951 by Jean Toomer. Used by permission of Liveright Publishing Corporation.

•"Ballad of Orange and Grape" Reprinted by permission of International Creative Management, Inc. Copyright © 2006 by Muriel Rukeyser.

•"One Art" from THE COMPLETE POEMS 1927-1979 by Elizabeth Bishop. Copyright © 1979, 1983 by Alice Helen Methfessel. Reprinted by permission of Farrar, Straus and Giroux, LLC.

Prestwick House, Inc., wishes to express our gratitude to the following poets who were kind enough to donate their poetry and allow us to use it in this anthology.

•"Hearts & Stones" © 2004 by Moira Egan. Reprinted by permission of the author. All rights reserved.

•"Lucy: BPM 3907" © 2004 by Moira Egan. Reprinted by permission of the author. All rights reserved.

•"Catching the Scent" © 1992 by Anne Haines. Reprinted by permission of the author. All rights reserved. "Catching the Scent" was originally published in *Sojourner*, Vol. 17 No. 9. May 1992.

•"Here. Now." © 2005 by Laurel K. Dodge. Reprinted by permission of the author. All rights reserved.

•"Beautiful Tie" © 2005 by Laurel K. Dodge. Reprinted by permission of the author. All rights reserved.

•"Tremor" © 2004 by Rebecca Loudon. Reprinted by permission of the author. All rights reserved.

•"Poem for a 75th Birthday" © 1999 by "Poetry" Magazine. Reprinted by permission of the author. All rights reserved.

•"The Blue Water Buffalo" © 2005 by Universities West Press. Reprinted by permission of the author. All rights reserved.

•"Pear" © 2006 by Eduardo C. Corral. Reprinted by permission of the author. All rights reserved.

•"First Tattoo" © 2005 by Tatyana Mishel. Reprinted by permission of the author. All rights reserved.

•"Euphonic Sounds" © 2006 by James Gurley. Reprinted by permission of the author. All rights reserved.

•"Stopping by 106th and Broadway © 2000-2001 by *Poet Lore*. Reprinted by permission of the author. All rights reserved.

•"Two Fish Stories" © 2005 by Steven D. Schroeder. Reprinted by permission of the author. All rights reserved.

•"Madeline Island" © 2006 by Teresa Ballard. Reprinted by permission of the author. All rights reserved.

•"Scar" © 2005 by Amy Lemmon. Originally appeared in *Prairie Schooner* (Vol. 79, No. 4, Winter 2005). Reprinted by permission of the author. All rights reserved.

•"Deciding on Quandary" © 1997 by Amy Lemmon. Originally appeared in Verse (Vol. 14, No. 2, Fall 1997). Reprinted by permission of the author. All rights reserved.

•"Work Ethics" by Emily Lloyd. Reprinted by permission of the author. All rights reserved.

•"XO" © 2006 by Paul Guest. Reprinted by permission of the author. All rights reserved.

In this book, you will study the art of the poem through an examination of what goes into each poem. Note the poet's use of words to show an emotion, to portray a situation, or to hint at the inexpressible that makes the poem unique.

INTRODUCTION

THE ART OF WRITING A POEM is a personal one that requires an author to communicate with readers on at least two levels. Readers should be able to understand the poem from a literal perspective—what happens in the poem— as well as a figurative one—what the poem means. The simplest types of poems communicate to us on these levels, and the more complex ones reach even deeper into our subconscious minds. While the cliché states that one picture is worth a thousand words, it is also quite true that one word can conjure up a thousand images. This is the essential nature of poetry—its Art.

Poetry is not, as many people think, a dying form of literary expression, one trailing into obsolescence. To refute that claim, this anthology offers many poems that were written in the twenty-first century. They are among the very best in this collection and are sure to inspire discussion about their construction and meaning. Older and better-known poems, however, have not been neglected. Your favorite poets—T. S. Eliot, Stephen Crane, William Shakespeare, Emily Dickinson, William Blake, E. E. Cummings, etc.—are included.

A critic once claimed that poetry is two things: a combination of words that define something precisely and a combination of words that leaves the meaning completely open to interpretation. A poet's use of words, therefore, is what makes a poem, not the length, the rhyme, the arrangement, or the meter. The examples in this anthology range in length from Ezra Pound's two-line "In a Station of the Metro" to Edgar Allan Poe's multi-paged "The Raven." Some rhyme and contain a specific meter, while others do not. Many contain poetic devices such as similes or alliteration; some are unadorned and simple. A few tell stories, several paint pictures, and others merely present a single image. Yet, they all fit that critic's definition of poetry. ❧

DISCOVERING GENRE:

Poetry

The Natural World

Dover Beach

MATTHEW ARNOLD

The sea is calm to-night.
The tide is full, the moon lies fair
Upon the straits; —on the French coast the light
Gleams and is gone; the cliffs of England stand,
Glimmering and vast, out in the tranquil bay.
Come to the window, sweet is the night air!
Only, from the long line of spray
Where the sea meets the moon-blanch'd land,
Listen! you hear the grating roar
Of pebbles which the waves draw back, and fling,
At their return, up the high strand,
Begin, and cease, and then again begin,
With tremulous cadence slow, and bring
The eternal note of sadness in.

Sophocles long ago
Heard it on the Aegean, and it brought
Into his mind the turbid ebb and flow
Of human misery; we
Find also in the sound a thought,
Hearing it by this distant northern sea.

Continued on next page

The Sea of Faith
Was once, too, at the full, and round earth's shore
Lay like the folds of a bright girdle furl'd.
But now I only hear
Its melancholy, long, withdrawing roar,
Retreating, to the breath
Of the night-wind, down the vast edges drear
And naked shingles of the world.

Ah, love, let us be true
To one another! for the world, which seems
To lie before us like a land of dreams,
So various, so beautiful, so new,
Hath really neither joy, nor love, nor light,

Nor certitude, nor peace, nor help for pain;
And we are here as on a darkling plain
Swept with confused alarms of struggle and flight,
Where ignorant armies clash by night.

Questions **Dover Beach**

1 Arnold uses a great deal of imagery to move the poem from a literal to a metaphoric level. Identify the images seen in the poem and discuss the metaphor that Arnold employs.

2 At the poem's beginning, Arnold describes the sea as "calm" and the air as "sweet." It is conversely the sound of the sea—the "grating roar"—that brings an "eternal note of sadness" into the first stanza and sets the tone for the rest of the poem. What does the poem suggest, then, about appearances?

3 Arnold's first two stanzas are melancholy and bittersweet. In the third stanza, he employs a metaphor that might explain this melancholy. Identify and analyze this metaphor and what it might add to your interpretation of Arnold's poem.

When I Heard the Learn'd Astronomer

WALT WHITMAN

When I heard the learn'd astronomer,
When the proofs, the figures, were ranged in columns before me,
When I was shown the charts, the diagrams, to add, divide, and
  measure them,
When I sitting heard the learn'd astronomer where he lectured with
  much applause in the lecture room,
How soon unaccountable I became tired and sick,
Till rising and gliding out I wander'd off by myself,
In the mystical moist night-air, and from time to time,
Look'd up in perfect silence at the stars.

When I Heard the Learn'd Astronomer

1 Every time Whitman mentions the astronomer, he emphasizes that the man is "learn'd." Why do you think Whitman repeats that word, "learn'd," whenever he brings up the astronomer? Is it a gesture of respect?

2 What does this poem suggest about our attempts to "measure" and "chart" the workings of the natural world?

3 Compare the first four lines of the poem to the second four lines. How are they different? Why do you think Whitman created this subtle distinction?

A Noiseless Patient Spider

WALT WHITMAN

A noiseless patient spider,
I mark'd where on a little promontory it stood isolated,
Mark'd how to explore the vacant, vast surrounding,
It launched forth filament, filament, filament, out of itself.
Ever unreeling them, ever tirelessly speeding them.

And you O my soul where you stand,
Surrounded, detached, in measureless oceans of space,
Ceaselessly musing, venturing, throwing, seeking the spheres to
    connect them,
Till the bridge you will need be form'd, till the ductile anchor hold,
Till the gossamer thread you fling catch somewhere, O my soul.

A Noiseless
Patient Spider

1 What is the effect of the repetition of the word "filament" in the beginning: "It launched forth filament, filament, filament"? What would be lost if Whitman had instead written, "It launched forth filament after filament"?

2 What is the overall tone of this poem? What does the poem's speaker learn from watching the spider?

3 In the second stanza, the speaker compares the searching of his soul to a spider's tentative exploration. What is he saying about his soul? The speaker seems, additionally, somewhat bewildered by what he has witnessed of the spider's exploration. Explain his confusion.

4 How does Whitman link structure to sense with his stanza break?

Lucy: BPM 3709*

M O I R A   E G A N

Astronomers had always theorized
that when a star's used up its nuclear fuel
and died, its carbon heart would crystallize.
And now they've found the proof: a cosmic jewel
ten billion trillion trillion carats' worth
of diamond in the sky: yes, like the song.
And when they seismographed the white dwarf's depths
she sang back, resonating like a gong.

Was that what I was hearing all those times
I walked at night to listen to the stars?
Just Lucy's music, a sidereal chime
that rang its way into my carbon heart?
I like the thought that burnt-out hearts of stars
can sing to us, even across light years.

*NOTE: The *Lucy* in the poem, whose scientific name is BPM 3709, is a star discovered in 2004, unique in that it is actually a diamond—a chunk of crystallized carbon. It was named "Lucy" after The Beatles' song "Lucy in the Sky with Diamonds."

Questions

Lucy: BPM 3709

1 In contrast to Whitman's "When I Heard the Learn'd Astronomer," Egan's poem takes its inspiration from astronomy and scientific discovery. What would you say is the theme of Egan's poem?

2 Many of the end-rhymes in Egan's poem are perfect rhymes—that is, they rhyme exactly: fuel/jewel, song/gong, and so on. The final two lines, or couplet, are an example of slant rhyme. Consider the effect of ending a poem with a slant rhyme. How would the poem's tone differ if Egan had ended with a perfect rhyme?

3 In the structural shift from the first to the second stanza, Egan's poem also shifts thematically. Identify this shift.

In Just-

E.E. CUMMINGS

in Just-
spring   when the world is mud-
luscious the little
lame balloonman

whistles   far   and wee

and eddyandbill come
running from marbles and
piracies and it's
spring

when the world is puddle-wonderful

the queer
old balloonman whistles
far   and   wee
and bettyandisabel come dancing

from hop-scotch and jump-rope and

it's
spring
and
          the

goat-footed

balloonMan   whistles
far
and
wee

Questions
In Just-

1 Cummings is one of the more unconventional and experimental poets in this collection, but the fact that he does not write in traditional lines does not mean that he breaks his lines at random intervals. Much thought is put into which words to leave alone on one line, how to space words and lines, and so on. That said, why do you think Cummings decided to run the children's names together as he did? What effect does he achieve with this technique?

2 In describing the season, Cummings invents new words by joining two together and coining others: mud-luscious, puddle-wonderful, for example. What tone do these invented words give to the poem?

3 What contrasts can you find in Cummings' poem? What do you think his purpose in including these contrasts was?

Oread

H . D .

Whirl up, sea—
whirl your pointed pines,
splash your pointed pines
on our rocks,
hurl your green over us,
cover us with your pools of fir.

Questions Oread

1. "Oread" is an extremely short poem with no significant rhyme scheme or meter. H.D. does, however, use other sound devices in the poem. How do the repetition (such as with the phrase "pointed pines"), alliteration (again, "pointed pines"), and internal rhyme ("whirl" and "hurl") contribute to the overall tone of the poem?

2. The resemblance of the sea to a pine forest is not one that would quickly spring to most of our minds, yet H.D. manages to make the association seem natural in very few lines. How does she achieve this? What makes the speaker's voice sound authoritative?

3. "Oread" is a prime example of a type of poetry known as imagism, which is characterized by brevity and directness of expression and simple, precise images. How does H.D. manage to show, rather than tell, the message of her poem? What is the message conveyed by "Oread"?

Garden
H . D .

I.

You are clear
O rose, cut in rock,
hard as the descent of hail.

I could scrape the color
from the petals
like spilt dye from a rock.

If I could break you
I could break a tree.

If I could stir
I could break a tree—
I could break you.

II.

O wind, rend open the heat,
cut apart the heat,
rend it to tatters.

Fruit cannot drop
through this thick air—
fruit cannot fall into the heat
that presses up and blunts
the points of pears
and rounds the grapes.

Cut the heat—
plough through it,
turning it on either side
of your path.

Questions **Garden**

1 In what way is "Garden" an Imagist poem? Describe the imagery found in the two sections of the poem and explain what links the two very different images.

2 "Garden" is full of fairly harsh sounding, one-syllable words: "cut," "scrape," "split," "break," "plough," and "rend." How do these affect the poem's tone?

3 In the second stanza, how does H.D. portray grapes and pears before the heat works on them? How does this image contribute to the cumulative portrait of heat as something "thick" and capable of being rent "to tatters"?

The Fish

MARIANNE MOORE

wade
through black jade.
Of the crow-blue mussel-shells, one keeps
     adjusting the ash-heaps;
         opening and shutting itself like

an
injured fan.
The barnacles which encrust the side
of the wave, cannot hide
there for the submerged shafts of the

sun,
split like spun
glass, move themselves with spotlight swiftness
     into the crevices—
         in and out, illuminating

the
turquoise sea
of bodies. The water drives a wedge
     of iron throughout the iron edge
         of the cliff; whereupon the stars,

pink
rice-grains, ink-
bespattered jelly fish, crabs like green
　　　lilies, and submarine
　　　　　　toadstools, slide each on the other.

All
external
marks of abuse are present on this
　　　defiant edifice—
　　　　　　all the physical features of

ac-
cident—lack
of cornice, dynamite grooves, burns, and
hatchet strokes, these things stand
out on it; the chasm-side is

dead.
Repeated
evidence has proved that it can live
on what can not revive
its youth. The sea grows old in it.

Continued on next page

Questions

1 Comment on the form of the poem. Where is there rhyme in the stanzas? Is the poem in any particular meter? In what way are the stanzas similar? What does the shape of the poem suggest?

2 What is the "defiant edifice" Moore mentions in the sixth stanza? What does the poem suggest about the relationship of the sun to the sea and the sea to the cliff? What does it suggest about fish?

3 In "The Fish," Moore creates a peculiar dichotomy of endurance and destruction in the relationship among the sea and the fish and the cliff. How does Moore manage to convey that the sea is capable of both a nurturing and destructive relationship to fish and cliff?

Thirteen Ways of Looking at a Blackbird

WALLACE STEVENS

I

Among twenty snowy mountains,
The only moving thing
Was the eye of the blackbird.

II

I was of three minds,
Like a tree
In which there are three blackbirds.

III

The blackbird whirled in the autumn winds.
It was a small part of the pantomime.

IV

A man and a woman
Are one.
A man and a woman and a blackbird
Are one.

V

I do not know which to prefer,
The beauty of inflections
Or the beauty of innuendoes,
The blackbird whistling
Or just after.

VI

Icicles filled the long window
With barbaric glass.
The shadow of the blackbird
Crossed it, to and fro.
The mood
Traced in the shadow
An indecipherable cause.

Continued on next page

VII

O thin men of Haddam,
Why do you imagine golden birds?
Do you not see how the blackbird
Walks around the feet
Of the women about you?

VIII

I know noble accents
And lucid, inescapable rhythms;
But I know, too,
That the blackbird is involved
In what I know.

IX

When the blackbird flew out of sight,
It marked the edge
Of one of many circles.

X

At the sight of blackbirds
Flying in a green light,
Even the bawds of euphony
Would cry out sharply.

XI

He rode over Connecticut
In a glass coach.
Once, a fear pierced him,
In that he mistook
The shadow of his equipage
For blackbirds.

XII

The river is moving.
The blackbird must be flying.

XIII

It was evening all afternoon.
It was snowing
And it was going to snow.
The blackbird sat
In the cedar-limbs.

Questions
Thirteen Ways of Looking at a Blackbird

1 Many of Stevens' "ways" of looking at a blackbird are reminiscent of haiku. Their language is unadorned, and they seem to be both quiet and mysterious bites of wisdom. Yet, other stanzas contrast with these. They are shorter or longer and deal with subjects far afield from a simple bird. Why is this? Which "ways" stand out from these, stylistically? That is, which do not seem quiet and contemplative, but active, or even aggressive? In your opinion, does having competing styles in the same poem "work"? What does it add? What does it take away?

2 Describe some of the images, techniques, and thoughts that Stevens uses in this poem.

3 Like "Oread," this poem is an example of Imagist verse, in which the poet's message is conveyed through carefully selected images and precise, minimal wording. What repeating image unifies the thirteen divisions of the poem? What are some of the different forms this image takes?

Fog

CARL SANDBURG

The fog comes
on little cat feet.
It sits looking
over harbor and city
on silent haunches
and then moves on.

Questions

1 This is a quiet, hushed poem. How does the tone complement the subject matter?

2 Comment on the poem's last line. How does it extend the poem beyond the boundaries of its six short lines?

3 Explain the effect of the extended metaphor that makes up this poem.

For I Will Consider My Cat Jeoffry

CHRISTOPHER SMART

For I will consider my Cat Jeoffry.
For he is the servant of the Living God duly and daily serving him.
For at the first glance of the glory of God in the East he worships in his
    way.
For this is done by wreathing his body seven times round with elegant
    quickness.
For then he leaps up to catch the musk, which is the blessing of God upon
    his prayer.
For he rolls upon prank to work it in.
For having done duty and received blessing he begins to consider himself.
For this he performs in ten degrees.
For first he looks upon his forepaws to see if they are clean.
For secondly he kicks up behind to clear away there.
For thirdly he works it upon stretch with the forepaws extended.
For fourthly he sharpens his paws by wood.
For fifthly he washes himself.
For sixthly he rolls upon wash.
For seventhly he fleas himself, that he may not be interrupted upon the
    beat.
For eighthly he rubs himself against a post.
For ninthly he looks up for his instructions.
For tenthly he goes in quest of food.
For having consider'd God and himself he will consider his neighbour.
For if he meets another cat he will kiss her in kindness.
For when he takes his prey he plays with it to give it a chance.
For one mouse in seven escapes by his dallying.

For when his day's work is done his business more properly begins.

For he keeps the Lord's watch in the night against the adversary.

For he counteracts the powers of darkness by his electrical skin and
glaring eyes.

For he counteracts the Devil, who is death, by brisking about the life.

For in his morning orisons he loves the sun and the sun loves him.

For he is of the tribe of Tiger.

For the Cherub Cat is a term of the Angel Tiger.

For he has the subtlety and hissing of a serpent, which in goodness he
suppresses.

For he will not do destruction, if he is well-fed, neither will he spit without
provocation.

For he purrs in thankfulness, when God tells him he's a good Cat.

For he is an instrument for the children to learn benevolence upon.

For every house is incomplete without him and a blessing is lacking in the
spirit.

For the Lord commanded Moses concerning the cats at the departure of
the Children of Israel from Egypt.

For every family had one cat at least in the bag.

For the English Cats are the best in Europe.

For he is the cleanest in the use of his forepaws of any quadruped.

For the dexterity of his defense is an instance of the love of God to him
exceedingly.

For he is the quickest to his mark of any creature.

For he is tenacious of his point.

For he is a mixture of gravity and waggery.

For he knows that God is his Saviour.

For there is nothing sweeter than his peace when at rest.

For there is nothing brisker than his life when in motion.

For he is of the Lord's poor and so indeed is he called by benevolence
perpetually—Poor Jeoffry! poor Jeoffry! the rat has bit thy throat.

For I bless the name of the Lord Jesus that Jeoffry is better.

For the divine spirit comes about his body to sustain it in complete cat.

For his tongue is exceeding pure so that it has in purity what it wants in
music.

For he is docile and can learn certain things.

For he can set up with gravity which is patience upon approbation.

For he can fetch and carry, which is patience in employment.

Continued on next page

For he can jump over a stick which is patience upon proof positive.

For he can spraggle upon waggle at the word of command.

For he can jump from an eminence into his master's bosom.

For he can catch the cork and toss it again.

For he is hated by the hypocrite and miser.

For the former is afraid of detection.

For the latter refuses the charge.

For he camels his back to bear the first notion of business.

For he is good to think on, if a man would express himself neatly.

For he made a great figure in Egypt for his signal services.

For he killed the Ichneumon-rat very pernicious by land.

For his ears are so acute that they sting again.

For from this proceeds the passing quickness of his attention.

For by stroking of him I have found out electricity.

For I perceived God's light about him both wax and fire.

For the Electrical fire is the spiritual substance, which God sends from heaven to sustain the bodies both of man and beast.

For God has blessed him in the variety of his movements.

For, though he cannot fly, he is an excellent clamberer.

For his motions upon the face of the earth are more than any other quadruped.

For he can tread to all the measures upon the music.

For he can swim for life.

For he can creep.

For I Will Consider My Cat Jeoffry

1 The use of the same phrase or word (for example, "For he can") at the beginning of successive stanzas is called anaphora. It is a device used more often by orators and speech-writers than it is by poets. What tone does Smart's use of anaphora impart to the poem?

2 In what way is this a religious poem, a song of praise for more than Jeoffrey?

3 What devices make this a poem, rather than merely a prosaic ramble about a cat?

The Eagle

ALFRED, LORD TENNYSON

He clasps the crag with crooked hands;
Close to the sun in lonely lands,
Ringed with the azure world, he stands.

The wrinkled sea beneath him crawls;
He watches from his mountain walls,
And like a thunderbolt he falls.

The Eagle

1 Two set-off lines of metered verse are called a couplet; three are called a tercet. Rarely does one see a tercet in which all three lines rhyme, and this poem is composed of two such tercets. How does this "stacked" rhyme influence the poem's tone?

2 What is the intended effect of the alliteration in the first tercet (clasps/crag/crooked/close, lonely/lands, for example)?

3 The last line of Tennyson's poem is an ambiguous one. Is the eagle's "fall" a power-filled dive toward some prey, or actually a fall aided by gravity? Explain your choice.

Lines Written in Early Spring

WILLIAM WORDSWORTH

I heard a thousand blended notes,
While in a grove I sat reclined,
In that sweet mood when pleasant thoughts
Bring sad thoughts to the mind.

To her fair works did Nature link
The human soul that through me ran;
And much it grieved my heart to think
What man has made of man.

Through primrose tufts, in that green bower,
The periwinkle trailed its wreaths;
And 'tis my faith that every flower
Enjoys the air it breathes.

The birds around me hopped and played,
Their thoughts I cannot measure:—
But the least motion which they made
It seemed a thrill of pleasure.

The budding twigs spread out their fan,
To catch the breezy air;
And I must think, do all I can,
That there was pleasure there.

If this belief from heaven be sent,
If such be Nature's holy plan,
Have I not reason to lament
What man has made of man?

Questions
Lines Written in Early Spring

1 What is the main idea of Wordsworth's poem? What is he saying about the natural world versus the social or industrial one?

2 Does Wordsworth's view of nature seem complete and well informed, or rosy and one-dimensional? Does his argument convince you?

3 How would you describe the form and rhythm of Wordsworth's poem? How does it echo the tone of the poem?

The Lake Isle of Innisfree

W . B .   Y E A T S

I will arise and go now, and go to Innisfree,
And a small cabin build there, of clay and wattles made;
Nine bean rows will I have there, a hive for the honeybee,
And live alone in the bee-loud glade.

And I shall have some peace there, for peace comes dropping slow,
Dropping from the veils of the morning to where the cricket sings;
There midnight's all a-glimmer, and noon a purple glow,
And evening full of the linnet's wings.

I will arise and go now, for always night and day
I hear the water lapping with low sounds by the shore;
While I stand on the roadway, or on the pavements gray,
I hear it in the deep heart's core.

Questions
The Lake Isle of Innisfree

1 Compare and contrast "The Lake Isle of Innisfree" with Wordsworth's "Lines Written in Early Spring." Both describe the peace found in natural settings. One makes a personal statement and the other a larger, political statement. If we can speak of goals in poetry, each poet has a different goal for his poem. Which is which? Which of the two poems do you think best achieves its goal?

2 What is "Innisfree"?

3 What do the last two lines tell you about the speaker? With these lines, what statement do you think Yeats might be making about urban and country life?

DISCOVERING GENRE:

Poetry

Technology and City Life

Preludes

T. S. ELIOT

I

The winter evening settles down
With smell of steaks in passageways.
Six o'clock.
The burnt-out ends of smoky days.
And now a gusty shower wraps
The grimy scraps
Of withered leaves about your feet
And newspapers from vacant lots;
The showers beat
On broken blinds and chimneypots,
And at the corner of the street
A lonely cab-horse steams and stamps.
And then the lighting of the lamps.

II

The morning comes to consciousness
Of faint stale smells of beer
From the sawdust-trampled street
With all its muddy feet that press
To early coffee-stands.
With the other masquerades
That time resumes,
One thinks of all the hands
That are raising dingy shades
In a thousand furnished rooms.

Continued on next page

III

You tossed a blanket from the bed
You lay upon your back, and waited;
You dozed, and watched the night revealing
The thousand sordid images
Of which your soul was constituted;
They flickered against the ceiling.
And when all the world came back
And the light crept up between the shutters
And you heard the sparrows in the gutters,
You had such a vision of the street
As the street hardly understands;
Sitting along the bed's edge, where
You curled the papers from your hair,
Or clasped the yellow soles of feet
In the palms of both soiled hands.

IV

His soul stretched tight across the skies
That fade behind a city block,
Or trampled by insistent feet
At four and five and six o'clock;
And short square fingers stuffing pipes,
And evening newspapers, and eyes
Assured of certain certainties,
The conscience of a blackened street
Impatient to assume the world.

I am moved by fancies that are curled
Around these images, and cling:
The notion of some infinitely gentle
Infinitely suffering thing.

Wipe your hand across your mouth, and laugh;
The worlds revolve like ancient women
Gathering fuel in vacant lots.

Questions
Preludes

1 A "prelude" is defined as the beginning of something, an introduction of sorts. Eliot's poem is arranged in a series of sections titled with Roman numerals. How is each section of the poem a prelude? To what is each a prelude?

2 One key characteristic of Eliot's poem is use of repetition. An example of this is with his use of the word "and" (particularly in the first and fourth stanzas), which, as a conjunction, tends to be used frequently in normal speech. When used excessively in print, however, it takes on a significance all its own. What do you think is Eliot's purpose in the repetition of "and"?

3 What comment is Eliot making about the individual in the second numbered part through the lines "One thinks of all the hands / That are raising dingy shades / In a thousand furnished rooms"?

A Rhyme About an Electrical Advertising Sign

VACHEL LINDSAY

I look on the specious electrical light
Blatant, mechanical, crawling and white,
Wickedly red or malignantly green
Like the beads of a young Senegambian queen.
Showing, while millions of souls hurry on,
The virtues of collars, from sunset till dawn,
By dart or by tumble of whirl within whirl,
Starting new fads for the shame-weary girl,
By maggotry motions in sickening line
Proclaiming a hat or a soup or a wine,
While there far above the steep cliffs of the street

The stars sing a message elusive and sweet.
Now man cannot rest in his pleasure and toil
His clumsy contraptions of coil upon coil
Till the thing he invents, in its use and its range,
Leads on to the marvelous CHANGE BEYOND CHANGE
Some day this old Broadway shall climb to the skies,
As a ribbon of cloud on a soul-wind shall rise.
And we shall be lifted, rejoicing by night,
Till we join with the planets who choir their delight.
The signs in the street and the signs in the skies
Shall make me a Zodiac, guiding and wise,
And Broadway make one with that marvelous stair
That is climbed by the rainbow-clad spirits of prayer.

A Rhyme About an Electrical Advertising Sign

1 What do you notice about the poem's meter, rhyme scheme, and use of words?

2 The title suggests a certain levity in the topic of this poem, as does the rhyme scheme and measured beat. After reading the poem, do you think Lindsay's message is one of humor and ease, or is it something different and more serious? Explain.

3 Why does Lindsay capitalize "CHANGE BEYOND CHANGE"?

City Trees

E D N A   S T .   V I N C E N T   M I L L A Y

The trees along this city street
Save for the traffic and the trains,
Would make a sound as thin and sweet
As trees in country lanes.

And people standing in their shade
Out of a shower, undoubtedly
Would hear such music as is made
Upon a country tree.

Oh, little leaves that are so dumb
Against the shrieking city air,
I watch you when the wind has come,—
I know what sound is there.

City Trees

1 What comparison does Millay draw between trees in the city and trees of the country?

2 What characteristics of form make this poem song-like?

3 What do you think Millay's message is?

In a Station
of the Metro

EZRA POUND

The apparition of these faces in the crowd;
Petals on a wet, black bough.

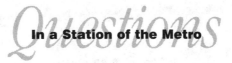

In a Station of the Metro

1 Pound's poem is one written in the Imagist tradition. Much like several others in this collection, it operates primarily on the power of the image. Describe the images Pound uses. Why do they work so effectively? What types of grammatical structures are present?

2 How does the word "apparition" serve to propel forward what could essentially be a simple statement of comparison to something more profound?

3 This particular poem of Pound's has often been categorized as a form of haiku, despite its non-traditional syllable arrangement. What, exactly, is a haiku, and how does Pound's poem fit the general description?

Chicago

CARL SANDBURG

HOG Butcher for the World,
Tool Maker, Stacker of Wheat,
Player with Railroads and the Nation's Freight Handler;
Stormy, husky, brawling,
City of the Big Shoulders:

They tell me you are wicked and I believe them, for I have seen your
painted women under the gas lamps luring the farm boys.
And they tell me you are crooked and I answer: Yes, it is true I have seen
the gunman kill and go free to kill again.
And they tell me you are brutal and my reply is: On the faces of women
and children I have seen the marks of wanton hunger.
And having answered so I turn once more to those who sneer at this my
city, and I give them back the sneer and say to them:
Come and show me another city with lifted head singing so proud to be
alive and coarse and strong and cunning.
Flinging magnetic curses amid the toil of piling job on job, here is a tall
bold slugger set vivid against the little soft cities;
Fierce as a dog with tongue lapping for action, cunning as a savage pitted
against the wilderness,
> Bareheaded,
> Shoveling,
> Wrecking,
> Planning,
> Building, breaking, rebuilding.
Under the smoke, dust all over his mouth, laughing with white teeth,
Under the terrible burden of destiny laughing as a young man laughs,
Laughing even as an ignorant fighter laughs who has never lost a battle,
Bragging and laughing that under his wrist is the pulse, and under his ribs
the heart of the
people
> Laughing!
Laughing the stormy, husky, brawling laughter of Youth, half-naked, sweat-
ing, proud to be Hog Butcher, Tool Maker, Stacker of Wheat, Player with
Railroads and Freight Handler to the Nation.

Questions

Chicago

1. How is Chicago personified? What personality traits does it acquire through this personification?

2. Describe the form Sandburg uses for this poem. Does it display any formal structure or traditional metrical pattern? Why do you think Sandburg chose to write the poem as he did?

3. Despite the wickedness, crookedness, and brutality of Chicago, the speaker offers a "sneer" to those who would defame it, and defends it instead. What is there, according to the speaker, that is worth defending?

To a Locomotive in Winter

WALT WHITMAN

Thee for my recitative,
Thee in the driving storm even as now, the snow, the winter-day declining,
Thee in thy panoply, thy measur'd dual throbbing and thy beat convulsive,
Thy black cylindric body, golden brass and silvery steel,
Thy ponderous side-bars, parallel and connecting rods, gyrating, shuttling at
     thy sides,
Thy metrical, now swelling pant and roar, now tapering in the distance,
Thy great protruding headlight fix'd in front,
Thy long, pale, floating vapor-pennants, tinged with delicate purple,
The dense and murky clouds out-belching from thy smoke-stack,
Thy knitted frame, thy springs and valves, the tremulous twinkle of thy
     wheels,
Thy train of cars behind, obedient, merrily following,
Through gale or calm, now swift, now slack, yet steadily careening;
Type of the modern – emblem of motion and power – pulse of the
     continent,
For once come serve the Muse and merge in verse, even as here I see thee,
With storm and buffeting gusts of wind and falling snow,
By day thy warning ringing bell to sound its notes,
By night thy silent signal lamps to swing.

Fierce-throated beauty!
Roll through my chant with all thy lawless music, thy swinging lamps at
     night,
Thy madly-whistled laughter, echoing, rumbling like an earthquake, rousing
     all,
Law of thyself complete, thine old track firmly holding,
(No sweetness debonair of tearful harp or glib piano thine,)
Thy trills and shrieks by rocks and hills return'd,
Launch'd o'er the prairies wide, across the lakes,
To the free skies unpent and glad and strong.

To a Locomotive in Winter

1 How does Whitman connect the attributes of a locomotive to the poem?

2 How does Whitman give the locomotive a character of sorts?

3 Why do you think Whitman chose to celebrate the locomotive in a poem? Identify a line or two that supports your response.

DISCOVERING GENRE:

Poetry

Society

Miniver Cheevy

EDWARD ARLINGTON ROBINSON

Miniver Cheevy, child of scorn,
  Grew lean while he assailed the seasons;
He wept that he was ever born,
  And he had reasons.

Miniver loved the days of old
  When swords were bright and steeds were prancing;
The vision of a warrior bold
  Would set him dancing.

Miniver sighed for what was not,
  And dreamed, and rested from his labors;
He dreamed of Thebes and Camelot,
  And Priam's neighbors.

Minever mourned the ripe renown
  That made so many a name so fragrant;
He mourned Romance, now on the town,
  And Art, a vagrant.

Miniver loved the Medici,
  Albeit he had never seen one;
He would have sinned incessantly
  Could he have been one.

Continued on next page

Miniver cursed the commonplace
        And eyed a khaki suit with loathing;
He missed the mediæval grace
        Of iron clothing.

Miniver scorned the gold he sought,
        But sore annoyed was he without it;
Miniver thought, and thought, and thought,
        And thought about it.

Miniver Cheevy, born too late,
        Scratched his head and kept on thinking;
Miniver coughed, and called it fate,
        And kept on drinking.

Miniver Cheevy

1 Do you think the poet feels sympathy toward Miniver, disgust toward Miniver, or both? Explain.

2 Robinson uses an effective blend of irony, humor, and empathy in describing Miniver Cheevy. Miniver reasons throughout the poem ("Miniver thought, and thought, and thought, / And thought about it.") that if he had just been born in a different time, he could have been an important person and done something special. He thinks that because he has not succeeded in his current time and place, it is not his fault—it is the *world* that is out of tune with him. Do you think Miniver would have been the success he imagines he would have been had he been born in a different age? How does Robinson use language to place doubt in the reader's mind that this could be the case?

3 What does the repetition of "and thought" in the seventh stanza accomplish? Why do you think Robinson repeated the phrase?

Richard Cory

EDWARD ARLINGTON ROBINSON

Whenever Richard Cory went down town,
We people on the pavement looked at him:
He was a gentleman from sole to crown,
Clean favored, and imperially slim.

And he was always quietly arrayed,
And he was always human when he talked;
But still he fluttered pulses when he said,
"Good-morning," and he glittered when he walked.

And he was rich—yes, richer than a king—
And admirably schooled in every grace;
In fine we thought that he was everything
To make us wish that we were in his place.

So on we worked, and waited for the light,
And went without the meat, and cursed the bread;
And Richard Cory, one calm summer night,
Went home and put a bullet through his head.

Richard Cory

1 What does "Richard Cory" suggest about how much we can know about people based on their appearance and behavior in social situations?

2 What does "Richard Cory" suggest about envy?

3 How does the word "calm" in the next-to-last line make the final line more surprising?

The Bean Eaters

GWENDOLYN BROOKS

They eat beans mostly, this old yellow pair.
Dinner is a casual affair.
Plain chipware on a plain and creaking wood,
Tin flatware.

Two who are Mostly Good.
Two who have lived their day,
But keep on putting on their clothes
And putting things away.

And remembering...
Remembering, with twinklings and twinges,
As they lean over the beans in their rented back room that
is full of beads and receipts and
dolls and cloths, tobacco crumbs, vases and fringes.

The Bean Eaters

1 Consider the form of "The Bean Eaters" and its ordinary language. How do the language and irregular rhyme work together?

2 "The Bean Eaters" is a portrait. How do you think the poet feels about her subjects, the couple? Where in the poem do you get the inklings of how she feels?

3 What effect does the capitalization of "Mostly Good" have? How would the poem's tone change if the phrase were not capitalized?

My Last Duchess

R O B E R T   B R O W N I N G

That's my last Duchess painted on the wall,
Looking as if she were alive. I call
That piece a wonder, now: Frà Pandolf's hands
Worked busily a day, and there she stands.
Will't please you sit and look at her? I said
"Frà Pandolf" by design, for never read
Strangers like you that pictured countenance,
The depth and passion of its earnest glance,
But to myself they turned (since none puts by
The curtain I have drawn for you, but I)
And seemed as they would ask me, if they durst,
How such a glance came there; so, not the first
Are you to turn and ask thus. Sir, 'twas not
Her husband's presence only, called that spot
Of joy into the Duchess' cheek: perhaps
Frà Pandolf chanced to say "Her mantle laps
Over my Lady's wrist too much," or "Paint
Must never hope to reproduce the faint
Half-flush that dies along her throat": such stuff
Was courtesy, she thought, and cause enough
For calling up that spot of joy. She had
A heart—how shall I say?—too soon made glad,
Too easily impressed; she liked whate'er
She looked on, and her looks went everywhere.
Sir, 'twas all one! My favour at her breast,
The dropping of the daylight in the West,
The bough of cherries some officious fool
Broke in the orchard for her, the white mule

She rode with round the terrace—all and each
Would draw from her alike the approving speech,
Or blush, at least. She thanked men,—good! but thanked
Somehow—I know not how—as if she ranked
My gift of a nine-hundred-years-old name
With anybody's gift. Who'd stoop to blame
This sort of trifling? Even had you skill
In speech—(which I have not)—to make your will
Quite clear to such an one, and say, "Just this
Or that in you disgusts me; here you miss,
Or there exceed the mark"—and if she let
Herself be lessoned so, nor plainly set
Her wits to yours, forsooth, and made excuse,
—E'en then would be some stooping, and I choose
Never to stoop. Oh sir, she smiled, no doubt,
Whene'er I passed her; but who passed without
Much the same smile? This grew; I gave commands;
Then all smiles stopped together. There she stands
As if alive. Will't please you rise? We'll meet
The company below, then. I repeat,
The Count your master's known munificence
Is ample warrant that no just pretence
Of mine for dowry will be disallowed;
Though his fair daughter's self, as I avowed
At starting, is my object. Nay, we'll go
Together down, sir. Notice Neptune, though,
Taming a sea-horse, thought a rarity,
Which Claus of Innsbruck cast in bronze for me!

My Last Dutchess

1 Although the poem is written in a series of couplets, it is an excellent example of a poem that should be read according to punctuation. Read the poem aloud, pausing or continuing as the punctuation directs instead of at the end of each line. What tone and effect does this give the poem?

2 In what ways does this poem tell us more about its speaker than it does about his late wife, the Duchess?

3 By the poem's end, the speaker has ceased speaking of the Duchess. Rather than end the poem there, Browning gives the speaker a few more seemingly insignificant lines; the speaker briefly describes another piece of art in his room. As the poem is called "My Last Duchess," why do you think Browning didn't end it with the last lines about her? What function do the last three lines serve?

The Love Song of J. Alfred Prufrock

T. S. ELIOT

S`io credesse che mia risposta fosse
A persona che mai tornasse al mondo,
Questa fiamma staria senza piu scosse.
Ma perciocche giammai di questo fondo
Non torno vivo alcun, s'i'odo il vero,
Senza tema d'infamia ti rispondo.

Let us go then, you and I,
When the evening is spread out against the sky
Like a patient etherized upon a table;
Let us go, through certain half-deserted streets,
The muttering retreats
Of restless nights in one-night cheap hotels
And sawdust restaurants with oyster-shells
Streets that follow like a tedious argument
Of insidious intent
To lead you to an overwhelming question...
Oh, do not ask, "What is it?"
Let us go and make our visit.

In the room the women come and go
Talking of Michelangelo.

The yellow fog that rubs its back upon the window-panes
The yellow smoke that rubs its muzzle on the window-panes;
Licked its tongue into the corners of the evening.
Lingered upon the pools that stand in drains.
Let fall upon its back the soot that falls from chimneys.
Slipped by the terrace, made a sudden leap,
And seeing that it was a soft October night,
Curled once about the house, and fell asleep.

Continued on next page

And indeed there will be time
For the yellow smoke that slides along the street,
Rubbing its back upon the window-panes;
There will be time, there will be time
To prepare a face to meet the faces that you meet;
There will be time to murder and create,
And time for all the works and days of hands
That lift and drop a question on your plate;
Time for you and time for me.
And time yet for a hundred indecisions,
And for a hundred visions and revisions,
Before the taking of a toast and tea.

In the room the women come and go
Talking of Michelangelo.

And indeed there will be time
To wonder, "Do I dare?" and "Do I dare?"
Time to turn back and descend the stair,
With a bald spot in the middle of my hair—
(They will say: "How his hair is growing thin!")
My morning coat, my collar mounting firmly to the chin,
My necktie rich and modest, but asserted by a simple pin—
(They will say: "But how his arms and legs are thin!")
Do I dare
Disturb the universe?
In a minute there is time
For decisions and revisions which a minute will reverse.

For I have known them all already, known them all:
Have known the evenings, mornings, afternoons,
I have measured out my life with coffee spoons;
I know the voices dying with a dying fall
Beneath the music from a farther room.
          So how should I presume?

And I have known the eyes already, known them all—
The eyes that fix you in a formulated phrase,
And when I am formulated, sprawling on a pin,
When I am pinned and wriggling on the wall,
Then how should I begin
To spit out all the butt-ends of my days and ways?
          And how should I presume?

And I have known the arms already, known them all—
Arms that are braceleted and white and bare
(But in the lamplight, downed with light brown hair!)
Is it perfume from a dress
That makes me so digress?
Arms that lie along a table, or wrap about a shawl.
      And should I then presume?
      And how should I begin?

.   .   .   .   .

Shall I say, I have gone at dusk through narrow streets
And watched the smoke that rises from the pipes
Of lonely men in shirt-sleeves, leaning out of windows?...

I should have been a pair of ragged claws
Scuttling across the floors of silent seas.

.   .   .   .   .

And the afternoon, the evening, sleeps so peacefully!
Smoothed by long fingers,
Asleep...tired...or it malingers,
Stretched on the floor, here beside you and me.
Should I, after tea and cakes and ices,
Have the strength to force the moment to its crisis?
But though I have wept and fasted, wept and prayed,
Though I have seen my head (grown slightly bald) brought in upon a platter,
I am no prophet—and here's no great matter;
I have seen the moment of my greatness flicker,
And I have seen the eternal Footman hold my coat, and snicker,
And in short, I was afraid.

And would it have been worth it, after all,
After the cups, the marmalade, the tea,
Among the porcelain, among some talk of you and me,
Would it have been worth while,
To have bitten off the matter with a smile,
To have squeezed the universe into a ball
To roll it toward some overwhelming question,
To say: "I am Lazarus, come from the dead,
Come back to tell you all, I shall tell you all"—
If one, settling a pillow by her head,
      Should say:"That is not what I meant at all.
      That is not it, at all."

Continued on next page

And would it have been worth it, after all,
Would it have been worth while,
After the sunsets and the dooryards and the sprinkled streets,
After the novels, after the teacups, after the skirts that trail along the floor—
And this, and so much more?—
It is impossible to say just what I mean!
But as if a magic lantern threw the nerves in patterns on a screen:
Would it have been worth while
If one, settling a pillow, or throwing off a shawl,
And turning toward the window, should say:
    "That is not it at all,
    That is not what I meant, at all."

   .   .   .   .   .

No! I am not Prince Hamlet, nor was meant to be;
Am an attendant lord, one that will do
To swell a progress, start a scene or two,
Advise the prince; no doubt, an easy tool,
Deferential, glad to be of use,
Politic, cautious, and meticulous;
Full of high sentence, but a bit obtuse;
At times, indeed, almost ridiculous—
Almost, at times, the Fool.

I grow old...I grow old...
I shall wear the bottoms of my trousers rolled.

Shall I part my hair behind? Do I dare to eat a peach?
I shall wear white flannel trousers, and walk upon the beach.
I have heard the mermaids singing, each to each.

I do not think that they will sing to me.

I have seen them riding seaward on the waves
Combing the white hair of the waves blown back
When the wind blows the water white and black.

We have lingered in the chambers of the sea
By sea-girls wreathed with seaweed red and brown
Till human voices wake us, and we drown.

The Love Song of J. Alfred Prufrock

1 Eliot's poem is an inquiry into the psyche of J. Alfred Prufrock, or, on a larger scale, the psyche of modern man. Having read it, how would you concisely describe Prufrock's situation and problem(s)? What is "wrong" with him?

2 The lines in Italian that serve as an epigraph to "Prufrock" are from Dante's *Inferno*. They are spoken by Guido da Montefeltro in response to the questions of Dante, whom Guido supposes is dead, since he (Dante) is in Hell (as a visitor). Encased in a flame, Guido says, "If I thought that I was replying to someone who would ever return to the world, this flame would cease to flicker. But since no one ever returns from these depths alive, if what I've heard is true, I will answer you without fear of infamy." What has this quotation to do with the speaker of "Prufrock"?

3 Consider Eliot's use of refrains ("In the room the women come and go / Talking of Michelangelo"; "That is not it, at all" etc.) in the poem. They might be indicative of either the monotony or the seeming impenetrability of the social scene Prufrock describes. "That is not it, at all" suggests the careless ease with which one might dismiss another's thoughts when one finally summons the courage to speak. What do the refrains add to the poem's meaning and to an understanding of Prufrock himself?

4 Is the drowning at the end of the poem literal? Explain.

"In the desert"

STEPHEN CRANE

In the desert
I saw a creature, naked, bestial,
Who, squatting upon the ground,
Held his heart in his hands,
And ate of it.
I said: "Is it good, friend?"
"It is bitter—bitter," he answered;
"But I like it
Because it is bitter,
And because it is my heart."

Questions "In the desert"

1 The speaker of this poem comes upon a gruesome scene, but his response is a casual "Is it good, friend?" What does this (especially the use of the word "friend") tell us about the speaker's own character?

2 What is the significance of the setting?

3 What does the fact that the creature "likes it" suggest about the nature of suffering or bitterness?

The Old Woman

JOSEPH CAMPBELL

As a white candle
In a holy place,
So is the beauty
Of an aged face.

As the spent radiance
Of the winter sun,
So is a woman
With her travail done.

Her brood gone from her,
And her thoughts as still
As the waters
Under a ruined mill.

The Old Woman

1 Trace the progression from stanza to stanza of the old woman. How does she change as the poem progresses, and how does the poem's form parallel this change? What is the dominant literary device the author employs?

2 How would the tone of "The Old Woman" differ if it ended with the second stanza? How does the third stanza change the poem's tone entirely?

3 Describe the images Campbell uses in this poem.

The Harlem Dancer

CLAUDE MCKAY

Applauding youths laughed with young prostitutes
And watched her perfect, half-clothed body sway;
Her voice was like the sound of blended flutes
Blown by black players upon a picnic day.
She sang and danced on gracefully and calm,
The light gauze hanging loose about her form;
To me she seemed a proudly-swaying palm
Grown lovelier for passing through a storm.
Upon her swarthy neck black shiny curls
Luxuriant fell; and tossing coins in praise,
The wine-flushed, bold-eyed boys, and even the girls,
Devoured her shape with eager, passionate gaze;
But looking at her falsely-smiling face,
I knew her self was not in that strange place.

Questions

The Harlem Dancer

1 "The Harlem Dancer" is written in the form of a Shakespearean sonnet. What is its rhyme scheme? One convention of this type of sonnet is to have a "turn" in the final couplet, so that the last two lines contain a twist or cast a different perspective on all that came before them. How successfully, in your opinion, does McKay exploit the possibility offered by this convention?

2 In one way, this sonnet is a kind of portrait. With words, it paints a picture of its subject, the Harlem Dancer. Describe the woman McKay creates with his words. What kind of woman is the dancer?

3 How do you think the speaker feels about the subject of this portrait? Is he immune to the dancer's physical charms? How does he differ from the other observers, if at all?

The River Merchant's Wife: A Letter

EZRA POUND

After Li Po

While my hair was still cut straight across my forehead
I played at the front gate, pulling flowers.
You came by on bamboo stilts, playing horse,
You walked about my seat, playing with blue plums.
And we went on living in the village of Chokan:
Two small people, without dislike or suspicion.

At fourteen I married My Lord you.
I never laughed, being bashful.
Lowering my head, I looked at the wall.
Called to, a thousand times, I never looked back.

At fifteen I stopped scowling,
I desired my dust to be mingled with yours
Forever and forever and forever.
Why should I climb the lookout?

At sixteen you departed,
You went into far Ku-to-en, by the river of swirling eddies,
And you have been gone five months.
The monkeys make sorrowful noise overhead.

You dragged your feet when you went out,
By the gate now, the moss is grown, the different mosses,
Too deep to clear them away!
The leaves fall early this autumn, in wind.
The paired butterflies are already yellow with August
Over the grass in the West garden;
They hurt me. I grow older.
If you are coming down through the narrows of the river Kiang,
Please let me know beforehand,
And I will come out to meet you
   As far as Cho-fu-sa.

The River Merchant's Wife: A Letter

1 Explain how Pound's word choices—for example, his use of some variation of "play" three times in the first section—effectively capture the stages of the couple's courtship as much as the descriptions of events and the wife's changing feelings do.

2 Like several of the other poems in this anthology, "The River Merchant's Wife: a Letter" is an example of Imagist poetry. Pound communicates the message and meaning of his poem through a series of simple, poignant images that are linked to the stages of their marriage and the woman's deepening feelings for her absent husband. What does Pound manage to communicate through this series of images? What is the effect of the images combined with his direct, simple language?

3 How do you think the "paired butterflies" "hurt" the wife?

Ozymandias

PERCY BYSSHE SHELLEY

I met a traveler from an antique land
Who said:"Two vast and trunkless legs of stone
Stand in the desert. Near them on the sand,
Half sunk, a shattered visage lies, whose frown
And wrinkled lip and sneer of cold command
Tell that its sculptor well those passions read
Which yet survive, stamped on these lifeless things,
The hand that mocked them and the heart that fed.
And on the pedestal these words appear:
'My name is Ozymandias, King of Kings:
Look on my works, ye mighty, and despair!'
Nothing beside remains. Round the decay
Of that colossal wreck, boundless and bare,
The lone and level sands stretch far away."

Questions

Ozymandias

1. What does the poem point out about greatness and power?

2. Identify the speakers in this poem. To whom is each one speaking?

3. There are two ways in which the scene the traveler describes might make the reader "despair"—one, of course, Ozymandias intended with his own words: that we should tremble in fear before his deeds and despair of ever conquering or achieving as much as he did. Why else might we feel despair at the site of the ruined statue with its engraved message and the emptiness surrounding it?

The Young Housewife

WILLIAM CARLOS WILLIAMS

At ten AM the young housewife
moves about in negligee behind
the wooden walls of her husband's house.
I pass solitary in my car.

Then again she comes to the curb
to call the ice-man, fish-man, and stands
shy, uncorseted, tucking in
stray ends of hair, and I compare her
to a fallen leaf.

The noiseless wheels of my car
rush with a crackling sound over
dried leaves as I bow and pass smiling.

The Young Housewife

1 How does the structure of this poem create a framework for the passing of time?

2 What do we learn about this poem's speaker from the poem? In what way is it as much a portrait of him as it is of the young housewife?

3 The speaker tells us that he compares the housewife to a fallen leaf, but does not elaborate on the comparison. What effect does this have on the poem's tone? What words contribute to the negative feeling in the poem?

4 Although the language of the poem and the nature of the speaker's interactions with the housewife are scrupulously polite and seemingly reserved, they seem to hint at some sexual awareness between the two, some level of desire, perhaps unacknowledged, that exists. How does Williams, with his matter-of-fact language, create this effect?

Hearts & Stones

MOIRA EGAN

for Coleman Hough

I have a friend who collects heart-shaped stones.
She plucks them out of nowhere, catching glints
and glimmers of this gift, the earth present-
ing chthonic* valentines to her alone.
Of marble, crystal, sandstone, fossil, quartz—
her vast collection spans a glacier's age.
It's said collectors are trying to assuage
a hole within, some awful primal loss.
If that's the case, I want to tell her that
we all have empty spaces, awful scars.
Even the earth accretes itself in layers;
that force creates both precious stones and granite.
And if her heart-shaped stones reflect the one inside,
I want to tell her every heart is petrified.

*The word chthonic (pronounced thonic) refers to spirits living within the earth.

Hearts & Stones

1 How does Egan's use of approximate and/or irregular rhyme and word choice affect the tone?

2 What is Egan suggesting about the earth when she writes that even it "accretes itself in layers"? What comparison does this image draw?

3 What is the literal meaning of the word "petrified" in the final line? What is its figurative meaning?

Mending Wall

ROBERT FROST

Something there is that doesn't love a wall,
That sends the frozen-ground-swell under it,
And spills the upper boulders in the sun;
And makes gaps even two can pass abreast.
The work of hunters is another thing:
I have come after them and made repair
Where they have left not one stone on a stone,
But they would have the rabbit out of hiding,
To please the yelping dogs. The gaps I mean,
No one has seen them made or heard them made,
But at spring mending-time we find them there.
I let my neighbor know beyond the hill;
And on a day we meet to walk the line
And set the wall between us once again.
We keep the wall between us as we go.
To each the boulders that have fallen to each.
And some are loaves and some so nearly balls
We have to use a spell to make them balance:
"Stay where you are until our backs are turned!"
We wear our fingers rough with handling them.
Oh, just another kind of out-door game,
One on a side. It comes to little more:
There where it is we do not need the wall:
He is all pine and I am apple orchard.
My apple trees will never get across
And eat the cones under his pines, I tell him.
He only says, "Good fences make good neighbors."
Spring is the mischief in me, and I wonder

If I could put a notion in his head:
"Why do they make good neighbors? Isn't it
Where there are cows? But here there are no cows.
Before I built a wall I'd ask to know
What I was walling in or walling out,
And to whom I was like to give offence.
Something there is that doesn't love a wall,
That wants it down." I could say "Elves" to him,
But it's not elves exactly, and I'd rather
He said it for himself. I see him there
Bringing a stone grasped firmly by the top
In each hand, like an old-stone savage armed.
He moves in darkness as it seems to me,
Not of woods only and the shade of trees.
He will not go behind his father's saying,
And he likes having thought of it so well
He says again, "Good fences make good neighbors."

Mending Wall

① Explain the significance of the line, "We keep the wall between us as we go."

② Though the speaker of the poem seems to think the wall unnecessary, he nevertheless meets his neighbor to repair it each spring. What does this tell us about him?

③ What are some of the images and techniques that Frost employs?

④ With which neighbor do you agree?

DISCOVERING GENRE:

Poetry

Politics and Struggle

Ballad of
Orange and Grape

MURIEL RUKEYSER

After you finish your work
after you do your day
after you've read your reading
after you've written your say—
you go down the street to the hot dog stand,
one block down and across the way.
On a blistering afternoon in East Harlem in the twentieth century.

Most of the windows are boarded up,
the rats run out of a sack—
sticking out of the crummy garage
one shiny long Cadillac;
at the glass door of the drug-addiction center,
a man who'd like to break your back.
But here's a brown woman with a little girl dressed in rose and pink, too.

Frankfurters frankfurters sizzle on the steel
where the hot-dog-man leans—
nothing else on the counter
but the usual two machines,
the grape one, empty, and the orange one, empty,
I face him in between.
A black boy comes along, looks at the hot dogs, goes on walking.

Continued on next page

I watch the man as he stands and pours
in the familiar shape
bright purple in the one marked ORANGE
orange in the one marked GRAPE,
the grape drink in the machine marked ORANGE
and orange drink in the GRAPE.
Just the one word large and clear, unmistakable, on each machine.

I ask him : How can we go on reading
and make sense out of what we read?—
How can they write and believe what they're writing,
the young ones across the street,
while you go on pouring grape into ORANGE
and orange into the one marked GRAPE—?
(How are we going to believe what we read and we write
 and we hear and we say and we do?)

He looks at the two machines and he smiles
and he shrugs and smiles and pours again.
It could be violence and nonviolence
it could be white and black women and men
it could be war and peace or any
binary system, love and hate, enemy, friend.
Yes and no, be and not-be, what we do and what we don't do.

On a corner in East Harlem
garbage, reading, a deep smile, rape,
forgetfulness, a hot street of murder,
misery, withered hope,
a man keeps pouring grape into ORANGE
and orange into the one marked GRAPE,
pouring orange into GRAPE and grape into ORANGE forever.

Ballad of Orange and Grape

1 Rukeyser titled her poem "Ballad of Orange and Grape." What elements lead a reader to conclude that this really is a balladic poem?

2 What is Rukeyser's fundamental problem with the man's error? What does it represent to her, in larger, more universal terms?

3 What is the man's reaction to the speaker's problem? Why is this significant?

Elegy in a Country Churchyard

G . K . CHESTERTON

The men that worked for England
They have their graves at home:
And birds and bees of England
About the cross can roam.

But they that fought for England,
Following a falling star,
Alas, alas for England
They have their graves afar.

And they that rule in England,
In stately conclave met,
Alas, alas for England
They have no graves as yet.

Elegy in a Country Churchyard

1 This poem mentions both war and death. Why do you think it appears in this section of the book, rather than in the section for "War" or "Death and Loss"?

2 What does the heavy use of metered rhythm do for the poem?

3 What is Chesterton's message in this poem?

The Golf Links

SARAH NORCLIFFE CLEGHORN

The golf links lie so near the mill
That almost every day
The laboring children can look out
And see the men at play.

The Golf Links

1 Does the brevity of the poem hinder or heighten the effect? Explain.

2 What contrast is presented?

3 What is the effect of the poem's rhyme, sound, and meter?

Incident

COUNTEE CULLEN

Once riding in old Baltimore,
Heart-filled, head-filled with glee,
I saw a Baltimorean
Keep looking straight at me.

Now I was eight and very small,
And he was no whit bigger,
And so I smiled, but he poked out
His tongue, and called me, "Nigger."

I saw the whole of Baltimore
From May until December;
Of all the things that happened there
That's all that I remember.

Questions — Incident

1 What effect do the rhyme and the short lines have on the tone of this poem?

2 How does the poem's format provide contrast to the poem's subject matter?

3 What comment is Cullen making about the impact of one negative experience as opposed to many positive experiences?

I Sit and Sew

ALICE DUNBAR-NELSON

I sit and sew—a useless task it seems,
My hands grown tired, my head weighed down with dreams—
The panoply of war, the martial tread of men,
Grim-faced, stern-eyed, gazing beyond the ken
Of lesser souls, whose eyes have not seen Death
Nor learned to hold their lives but as a breath—
But—I must sit and sew.

I sit and sew—my heart aches with desire—
That pageant terrible, that fiercely pouring fire
On wasted fields, and writhing grotesque things
Once men. My soul in pity flings
Appealing cries, yearning only to go
There in that holocaust of hell, those fields of woe—
But—I must sit and sew.—

The little useless seam, the idle patch;
Why dream I here beneath my homely thatch,
When there they lie in sodden mud and rain,
Pitifully calling me, the quick ones and the slain?
You need, me, Christ! It is no roseate seam
That beckons me—this petty futile seam,
It stifles me—God, must I sit and sew?

Questions

I Sit and Sew

1 What words reveal that the speaker believes that what she does, "sit and sew," is insignificant?

2 What does the speaker dream of as she sits and sews? What is her internal conflict?

3 Most of each stanza's lines are around ten syllables in length and are arranged in clearly defined rhyming couplets. The seventh line of each stanza, except the final stanza, is much shorter, with only six syllables. Why do you think Dunbar altered her meter and rhyme in this way? Why does she not do so in the final line of the poem, but instead reverts back to her ten syllables-per-line beat?

We Wear the Mask

PAUL LAURENCE DUNBAR

We wear the mask that grins and lies,
It hides our cheeks and shades our eyes,—
This debt we pay to human guile;
With torn and bleeding hearts we smile,
And mouth with myriad subtleties.

Why should the world be overwise,
In counting all our tears and sighs?
Nay, let them only see us, while
We wear the mask.

We smile, but, O great Christ, our cries
To thee from tortured souls arise.
We sing, but oh the clay is vile
Beneath our feet, and long the mile;
But let the world dream otherwise,
We wear the mask!

Questions

We Wear the Mask

1 This poem seems to be formal in its structure, particularly as it is written in iambic tetrameter. Why do you think Dunbar composed the poem in this manner? How does this help the poet get his message across?

2 For whom is this poem written? How do you know?

3 How is the poem itself "masked," as far as it subject is concerned? What does the "mask" suggest?

Sympathy

PAUL LAURENCE DUNBAR

I know what the caged bird feels, alas!
        When the sun is bright on the upland slopes;
When the wind stirs soft through the springing grass,
And the river flows like a stream of glass;
        When the first bird sings and the first bud opes,
And the faint perfume from its chalice steals—
I know what the caged bird feels!

I know why the caged bird beats his wing
        Till its blood is red on the cruel bars;
For he must fly back to his perch and cling
When he fain would be on the bough a-swing;
        And a pain still throbs in the old, old scars
And they pulse again with a keener sting—
I know why he beats his wing!

I know why the caged bird sings, ah me,
        When his wing is bruised and his bosom sore,—
When he beats his bars and he would be free;
It is not a carol of joy or glee,
        But a prayer that he sends from his heart's deep core,
But a plea, that upward to Heaven he flings—
I know why the caged bird sings!

Questions

Sympathy

1 How does Dunbar use repetition to frame his verse? Explain the metaphor of the "caged bird."

2 How do you interpret Dunbar's message in this poem? Can you think of more than one way to interpret it?

3 How does the tempo change slightly between the first and second stanzas? How does the author accomplish this, considering that the syllabic structure does not significantly alter?

The Negro Speaks of Rivers

LANGSTON HUGHES

I've known rivers:
I've known rivers ancient as the world and older than the
flow of human blood in human veins.

My soul has grown deep like the rivers.

I bathed in the Euphrates when dawns were young.
I build my hut near the Congo and it lulled me to sleep.
I looked upon the Nile and raised the pyramids above it.
I heard the singing of the Mississippi when Abe Lincoln
went down to New Orleans, and I've seen its muddy
bosom turn all golden in the sunset.

I've known rivers:
Ancient, dusky rivers.

My soul has grown deep like the rivers.

The Negro Speaks of Rivers

1 What do references to ideas such as sleep, sunset, and rivers that are "ancient" and "dusky" evoke? What is Hughes' message?

2 How would you characterize the form and diction of Hughes' poem? What techniques does Hughes use in the poem?

3 What is the purpose of the references to the ancient rivers of the Euphrates, the Congo, the Nile, and the Mississippi? What do they have in common?

The Man with the Hoe

EDWIN MARKHAM

Bowed by the weight of centuries he leans
Upon his hoe and gazes on the ground,
The emptiness of ages in his face,
And on his back the burden of the world.
Who made him dead to rapture and despair,
A thing that grieves not, and that never hopes,
Stolid and stunned, a brother to the ox?
Who loosened and let down this brutal jaw?
Whose was the hand that slanted back this brow?
Whose breath blew out the light within this brain?
Is this the Thing the Lord God made and gave
To have dominion over sea and land;
To trace the stars and search the heavens for power;
To feel the passion of eternity?
Is this the dream He dreamed who shaped the suns
And marked their ways upon the ancient deep?
Down all the caverns of Hell to their last gulf
There is no shape more terrible than this—
More tongued with cries against the world's blind greed—
More filled with signs and portents for the soul—
More packed with danger to the universe.
What gulfs between him and the seraphim!
Slave of the wheel of labor, what to him
Are Plato and the swing of the Pleiades?
What the long reaches of the peaks of song,
The rift of dawn, the reddening of the rose?
Through this dread shape the suffering ages look;
Time's tragedy is in that aching stoop;

Through this dread shape humanity betrayed,
Plundered, profaned, and disinherited,
Cries protest to the Powers that made the World,
A protest that is also prophecy.
O masters, lords and rulers in all lands,
Is this the handiwork you give to God,
This monstrous thing distorted and soul-quenched?
How will you ever straighten up this shape;
Touch it again with immortality;
Give back the upward looking and the light;
Rebuild in it the music and the dream;
Make right the immemorial infamies,
Perfidious wrongs, immedicable woes?
O masters, lords and rulers in all lands,
How will the Future reckon with this man?
How answer his brute question in that hour
When whirlwinds of rebellion shake all shores?
How will it be with kingdoms and with kings—
With those who shaped him to the thing he is—
When this dumb terror shall rise to judge the world,
After the silence of the centuries?

The Man with the Hoe

❶ In what ways is the figure depicted by Markham more animal than human?

❷ Markham's poem was written in response to a painting by Millet entitled "Man With a Hoe." In the painting, the farmer leans wearily on his hoe; his features are indistinct, and his clothes are ragged. The background is bleak, as is the land he is working. How do you think both the painting and the poem present a stark contrast to the often-romanticized ideal of the rural farmer and the benefits of his labor?

❸ What tone does Markham create with his vision of the man with the hoe? What word choices contribute to the tone?

DISCOVERING GENRE:
Poetry

War

War is Kind

S T E P H E N   C R A N E

Do not weep, maiden, for war is kind.
Because the lover threw wild hands toward the sky
And the affrighted steed ran on alone,
Do not weep.
War is kind.

Hoarse, booming drums of the regiment,
Little souls who thirst for fight,
These men were born to drill and die.
The unexplained glory flies above them,
Great is the Battle-God, great, and his Kingdom—
A field where a thousand corpses lie.

Do not weep, babe, for war is kind.
Because your father tumbled in the yellow trenches,
Raged at his breast, gulped and died,
Do not weep.
War is kind.

Continued on next page

Swift blazing flag of the regiment,
Eagle with crest of red and gold,
These men were born to drill and die.
Point for them the virtue of slaughter,
Make plain to them the excellence of killing
And a field where a thousand corpses lie.

Mother whose heart hung humble as a button
On the bright splendid shroud of your son,
Do not weep.
War is kind.

War is Kind

1 How would you describe the tone of this poem? Is the speaker really trying to convince those he addresses that war is "kind"?

2 What effect does the repetition of the phrase "These men were born to drill and die" achieve? How does the repetition mirror the phrase's content?

3 Though this poem may be seen as having a decidedly anti-war sentiment, Crane doesn't shy away from describing what might be considered war's "glamorous" aspects—for example, the "[s]wift blazing flag of the regiment," the "[e]agle with crest of red and gold," and the "booming drums of the regiment." Why do you think he includes these heart-stirring descriptions in the poem?

"Tell brave deeds of war"

S T E P H E N   C R A N E

"Tell brave deeds of war."

Then they recounted tales,—
"There were stern stands
And bitter runs for glory."

Ah, I think there were braver deeds.

"Tell brave deeds of war"

1 What do you think Crane means by this poem's last line? What "braver deeds" does he refer to?

2 Comment on the poem's narration and brevity.

Dreamers

SIEGFRIED SASSOON

Soldiers are citizens of death's gray land,
Drawing no dividend from time's tomorrows.
In the great hour of destiny they stand,
Each with his feuds, and jealousies, and sorrows.
Soldiers are sworn to action; they must win
Some flaming, fatal climax with their lives.
Soldiers are dreamers; when the guns begin
They think of firelit homes, clean beds, and wives.

I see them in foul dug-outs, gnawed by rats,
And in the ruined trenches, lashed with rain,
Dreaming of things they did with balls and bats,
And mocked by hopeless longing to regain
Bank-holidays, and picture shows, and spats,
And going to the office in the train.

Questions **Dreamers**

1 What does the juxtaposition of the military images and those related to a civilian lifestyle serve to accomplish?

2 How does this poem follow the Petrarchan sonnet tradition? Identify characteristics that make it a sonnet.

3 What words accurately portray the time or era that Sassoon describes?

4 What does Sassoon mean when he describes soldiers as "mocked by hopeless longing to regain / Bank-holidays, and picture shows, and spats, / And going to the office in the train"?

The Dug-Out

SIEGFRIED SASSOON

Why do you lie with your legs ungainly huddled,
And one arm bent across your sullen, cold,
Exhausted face? It hurts my heart to watch you,
Deep-shadowed from the candle's guttering gold;
And you wonder why I shake you by the shoulder;
Drowsy, you mumble and sigh and turn your head...
You are too young to fall asleep for ever;
And when you sleep you remind me of the dead.

The Dug-Out

1 Why does the speaker wake his slumbering comrade, even as he comments on the friend's "exhausted" state?

2 Why do you think Sassoon italicizes the last two lines? What point is he trying to drive home?

3 Compare and contrast this poem of Sassoon's with another in this collection, "Dreamers." Do you see any similarities or striking differences of tone?

Grass

CARL SANDBURG

Pile the bodies high at Austerlitz and Waterloo,
Shovel them under and let me work—
I am the grass; I cover all.

And pile them high at Gettysburg
And pile them high at Ypres and Verdun.
Shovel them under and let me work.
Two years, ten years, and passengers ask the conductor:
What place is this?
Where are we now?

I am the grass.
Let me work.

Questions

1 What does "Grass" suggest about the events that are significant to humankind versus the events that are significant to Nature?

2 Explain the poetic device Sandburg utilizes in this poem. What effect does it have on the readers' feelings regarding the subject matter?

3 How does the grass seem to feel about its "work"—and about people?

The Blue Water Buffalo

MARILYN L. TAYLOR

One in 250 Cambodians, or 40,000 people,
have lost a limb to a landmine.
—Newsfront, U.N. Development Programme
Communications Office

On both sides of the screaming highway, the world
is made of emerald silk—sumptuous bolts of it,
stitched by threads of water into cushions
that shimmer and float on the Mekong's munificent glut.

In between them plods the ancient buffalo—dark blue
in the steamy distance, and legless
where the surface of the ditch dissects
the body from its waterlogged supports below

or it might be a woman, up to her thighs
in the lukewarm ooze, bending at the waist
with the plain grace of habit, delving for weeds
in water that receives her wrist and forearm

as she feels for the alien stalk, the foreign blade
beneath that greenest of green coverlets
where brittle pods in their corroding skins
now shift, waiting to salt the fields with horror.

The Blue Water Buffalo

1 What poetic devices does Taylor use to make her poem interesting and compelling? Point out some contrasts in the poem.

2 Note the comparison of the water buffalo to the woman—"or it might be a woman, up to her thighs / in the lukewarm ooze." What comment do you think the author could be making here?

3 How does the poem shift with the last stanza?

There Will Come Soft Rains

SARA TEASDALE

There will come soft rains and the smell of the ground,
And swallows circling with their shimmering sound;

And frogs in the pools singing at night,
And wild plum-trees in tremulous white.

Robins will wear their feathery fire
Whistling their whims on a low fence-wire;

And not one will know of the war, not one
Will care at last when it is done.

Not one would mind, neither bird nor tree,
If mankind perished utterly;

And Spring herself, when she woke at dawn
Would scarcely know that we were gone.

There Will Come Soft Rains

1 What is the effect of alliteration in this poem, particularly in lines one, two, five, and six? What senses does Teasdale involve? How is the poem arranged?

2 Teasdale fills the first six lines with pastoral images; only in the seventh does she mention war. What is the effect of this delay, this slow approach to the actual point of the poem?

3 What do the last two lines reveal about the poet's message?

Dulce Et Decorum Est

WILFRED OWEN

Bent double, like old beggars under sacks,
Knock-kneed, coughing like hags, we cursed through sludge,
Till on the haunting flares we turned our backs
And towards our distant rest began to trudge.
Men marched asleep. Many had lost their boots
But limped on, blood-shod. All went lame; all blind;
Drunk with fatigue; deaf even to the hoots
Of disappointed shells that dropped behind.

GAS! Gas! Quick, boys!—An ecstasy of fumbling,
Fitting the clumsy helmets just in time;
But someone still was yelling out and stumbling
And floundering like a man in fire or lime.—
Dim, through the misty panes and thick green light
As under a green sea, I saw him drowning.

In all my dreams, before my helpless sight,
He plunges at me, guttering, choking, drowning.

If in some smothering dreams you too could pace
Behind the wagon that we flung him in,
And watch the white eyes writhing in his face,
His hanging face, like a devil's sick of sin;
If you could hear, at every jolt, the blood
Come gargling from the froth-corrupted lungs,
Obscene as cancer, bitter as the cud
Of vile, incurable sores on innocent tongues,—
My friend, you would not tell with such high zest
To children ardent for some desperate glory,
The old Lie: Dulce et decorum est
Pro patria mori.

Dulce Et Decorum Est

1 Owen describes the soldiers as "beggars" and "hags." Why do you think he employs such terms? Are they insults? Are they unpatriotic?

2 Translated into English, the final words of the poem read, "It is sweet and honorable to die for one's country." How does the rest of the poem belie this statement?

3 How would you describe Owen's tone in this poem? How does the final statement register with the tone? What other words or images aid Owen in establishing this tone.

Beat! Beat! Drums!

W A L T W H I T M A N

BEAT! beat! drums!—blow! bugles! blow!
Through the windows—through doors—burst like a ruthless force,
Into the solemn church, and scatter the congregation,
Into the school where the scholar is studying;
Leave not the bridegroom quiet—no happiness must he have now with his
   bride,
Nor the peaceful farmer any peace, ploughing his field or gathering his
   grain,
So fierce you whirr and pound you drums—so shrill you bugles blow.

Beat! beat! drums!—blow! bugles! blow!
Over the traffic of cities—over the rumble of wheels in the streets;
Are beds prepared for sleepers at night in the houses? no sleepers must
   sleep in those beds,
No bargainers' bargains by day—no brokers or speculators—would they
   continue?
Would the talkers be talking? would the singer attempt to sing?
Would the lawyer rise in the court to state his case before the judge?
Then rattle quicker, heavier drums—you bugles wilder blow.

Beat! beat! drums!—blow! bugles! blow!
Make no parley—stop for no expostulation,
Mind not the timid—mind not the weeper or prayer,
Mind not the old man beseeching the young man,
Let not the child's voice be heard, nor the mother's entreaties,
Make even the trestles to shake the dead where they lie awaiting the
   hearses,
So strong you thump O terrible drums—so loud you bugles blow.

Beat! Beat! Drums!

1 Identify the speaker of this poem and the message he is communicating. To whom is he speaking? How would you describe the tone of the poem?

2 How does the rhythm of Whitman's verse mirror the content of the verse?

3 How does Whitman communicate his ideas about war?

Reconciliation

WALT WHITMAN

Word over all, beautiful as the sky,
Beautiful that war and all its deeds of carnage must in time be utterly lost,
That the hands of the sisters Death and Night incessantly softly wash again,
      and ever again, this soil'd world;
For my enemy is dead—a man divine as myself is dead,
I look where he lies white-faced and still in the coffin—I draw near,
Bend down and touch lightly with my lips the white face in the coffin.

Questions
Reconciliation

1 Reread Carl Sandburg's poem "Grass," included in this section of the anthology. What concept do these two poems share? How are they different? Which do you find more effective, and why?

2 Consider Whitman's use of the word "enemy" in this poem. Why do you think he chooses to use it, since it seems clear that the speaker does not feel any personal animosity towards the dead man?

3 What is the "word over all, beautiful as the sky" and why is it so beautiful? What is Whitman's twofold message in this poem?

First Tattoo

TATYANA MISHEL

"You bleeding heart!" the tattoo artist laughed,
softly blowing dagger tips. The young man feels

a head-ache—wine-ache—fading, swings his feet
above the floor as pebbles rattle through his shoes
such young, young shoes. Twenty years un-old, he gets
a first impression: "This will make me, save me,"

whispers youth. Outside, the leaves of autumn press against
the cracked glass door. Regret—a word that does not yet

exist, nor does the war or carrying friends away to die beneath
palm trees, swaying in goodbyes; nor the three wives or

the tattoo scratched-out of Ruth. Two years from now, he will
kiss the salty underworld and know it, almost—

on a ship riding the Pacific, stars shivering
in their black beds, enemy planes crying for more sky.

He will touch the inky dagger at his nipple to remember
who he is and who he isn't—one heart, holy, barely breathing.

Questions

First Tattoo

❶ What scenario is suggested by the first three couplets?

❷ What does the fourth couplet and the ones that follow suggest about the decision the young man has made, and about the author's message as well?

❸ What does the tattoo signify?

DISCOVERING GENRE:

Poetry

Religion

Denial

GEORGE HERBERT

When my devotions could not pierce
    Thy silent ears;
Then was my heart broken, as was my verse;
   My breast was full of fears
    And disorder,

My bent thoughts, like a brittle bow,
    Did fly asunder:
Each took his way; some would to pleasures go,
   Some to the wars and thunder
    Of alarms.

"As good go any where," they say,
    "As to benumb
Both knees and heart, in crying night and day,
   Come, come, my God, O come,
    But no hearing."

O that thou shouldst give dust a tongue
    To cry to thee,
And then not hear it crying! all day long
   My heart was in my knee,
    But no hearing.

Continued on next page

Therefore my soul lay out of sight,
  Untuned, unstrung:
My feeble spirit, unable to look right,
 Like a nipped blossom, hung
   Discontented.

O cheer and tune my heartless breast,
  Defer no time;
That so thy favors granting my request,
 They and my mind may chime,
    And mend my rime.

Questions

Denial

1 Glance over the rhyme scheme of Herbert's "Denial." What do you note about the rhyme scheme that shifts in the last stanza? How does this seem to be echoed in the poet's message?

2 What is Herbert's message in "Denial"?

3 Where does the speaker seek solace for the disorder of his thoughts? What realization does he make in the fourth stanza regarding this?

Easter Wings

GEORGE HERBERT

Lord, Who createdst man in wealth and store,
Though foolishly he lost the same,
Decaying more and more,
Till he became
Most poore:

With Thee
O let me rise
As larks, harmoniously,
And sing this day Thy victories:
Then shall the fall further the flight in me.

My tender age in sorrow did beginne:
And still with sicknesses and shame
Thou didst so punish sinne,
That I became
Most thinne.

With Thee
Let me combine
And feel this day Thy victorie:
For, if I imp my wing on Thine,
Affliction shall advance the flight in me.

Easter Wings

1 Discuss the shape of the poem. How does shape tend to echo Herbert's meaning?

2 How does Herbert move from the general to the specific in the poem?

3 Look at the movement imagery in the poem and explain it.

God's Grandeur

G ERARD   M ANLEY   H OPKINS

The world is charged with the grandeur of God.
It will flame out, like shining from shook foil;
It gathers to a greatness, like the ooze of oil
Crushed. Why do men then now not reck his rod?
Generations have trod, have trod, have trod;
And all is seared with trade; bleared, smeared with toil;
And wears man's smudge and shares man's smell: the soil
Is bare now, nor can foot feel, being shod.

And for all this, nature is never spent;
There lives the dearest freshness deep down things;
And though the last lights off the black West went
Oh, morning, at the brown brink eastward, springs—
Because the Holy Ghost over the bent
World broods with warm breast and with ah! bright wings.

Questions

God's Grandeur

1 What failure does the speaker ascribe to mankind? What does mankind fail to recognize in nature?

2 How does the speaker use his description of nature to glorify God?

3 How does Hopkins use sound devices to give the poem a weighty, philosophical tone?

Pied Beauty

GERARD MANLEY HOPKINS

Glory be to God for dappled things,
   For skies of couple-color as a brinded cow,
      For rose-moles all in stipple upon trout that swim;
Fresh-firecoal chestnut-falls, finches' wings;
   Landscape plotted and pieced, fold, fallow and plough,
      And all trades, their gear and tackle and trim.

All things counter, original, spare, strange,
   Whatever is fickle, freckled (who knows how?)
      With swift, slow; sweet, sour; adazzle, dim.
He fathers-forth whose beauty is past change;
      Praise him.

Pied Beauty

1 What is Hopkins' subject in "Pied Beauty"?

2 How does this poem attempt to bring nature to the front of human consciousness?

3 How does the author's choice of things to describe in this poem, and the form as well, reinforce Hopkins' message of the beauty present in the diversity of God's creations?

The Tyger

WILLIAM BLAKE

Tyger! Tyger! burning bright
In the forests of the night,
What immortal hand or eye
Could frame thy fearful symmetry?

In what distant deeps or skies
Burnt the fire of thine eyes?
On what wings dare he aspire?
What the hand dare seize the fire?

And what shoulder, & what art
Could twist the sinews of thy heart?
And when thy heart began to beat,
What dread hand? & what dread feet?

What the hammer? what the chain?
In what furnace was thy brain?
What the anvil? what dread grasp
Dare its deadly terrors clasp?

When the stars threw down their spears,
And watered heaven with their tears,
Did he smile his work to see?
Did he who made the Lamb make thee?

Tyger! Tyger! burning bright
In the forests of the night,
What immortal hand or eye
Dare frame thy fearful symmetry?

Questions
The Tyger

1 There are numerous levels of meaning inherent in "The Tyger." On a literal level, what question do you think Blake is posing? On a different, more allegorical level, what do you think Blake is asking?

2 "The Tyger" ends without an answer to the question "What immortal hand or eye / Dare frame thy fearful symmetry." Why do you think Blake ends his poem without answering the question he poses?

3 Comment on the form of the poem. How is it arranged? What kind of rhyme scheme is present? What is the effect of these techniques?

E Tenebris*

OSCAR WILDE

Come down, O Christ, and help me! reach thy hand,
For I am drowning in a stormier sea
Than Simon on Thy lake of Galilee:
The wine of life is spilt upon the sand,
My heart is as some famine-murdered land,
Whence all good things have perished utterly,
And well I know my soul in Hell must lie
If I this night before God's throne should stand.
"He sleeps perchance, or rideth to the chase,
Like Baal, when his prophets howled that name
From morn to noon on Carmel's smitten height."
Nay, peace, I shall behold before the night,
The feet of brass, the robe more white than flame,
The wounded hands, the weary human face.

*from the darkness [of hell]

E Tenebris

1 The key to understanding this poem lies in understanding the biblical allusions to Simon and the lake of Galilee and Baal. Research these if you are unfamiliar with them and explain each.

2 Look at the form of this poem. Is it a sonnet? In what ways does it both fit the form of a sonnet and step outside the traditional form? What is the rhyme scheme?

3 What is the speaker's message in this poem?

Sonnet on Hearing the *Dies Irae* Sung in the Sistine Chapel

O SCAR   W ILDE

Nay, Lord, not thus! white lilies in the spring,
Sad olive-groves, or silver-breasted dove,
Teach me more clearly of Thy life and love
Than terrors of red flame and thundering.
The empurpled vines dear memories of Thee bring:
A bird at evening flying to its nest,
Tells me of One who had no place of rest:
I think it is of Thee the sparrows sing.
Come rather on some autumn afternoon,
When red and brown are burnished on the leaves,
And the fields echo to the gleaner's song,
Come when the splendid fulness of the moon
Looks down upon the rows of golden sheaves,
And reap Thy harvest: we have waited long.

Sonnet on Hearing the *Dies Irae* Sung in the Sistine Chapel

1 In his title, Wilde alludes to the "Dies Irae" and "the Sistine Chapel." Research and explain these allusions.

2 As with "E Tenebris," Wilde takes liberties with the traditional sonnet form. Do you think his close but imprecise use of the sonnet form adds or detracts from the poem? Explain your response.

3 Explain the "turn," and subsequently Wilde's message, in this poem.

DISCOVERING GENRE:

Poetry

Emotion

Jealousy

RUPERT BROOKE

When I see you, who were so wise and cool,
Gazing with silly sickness on that fool
You've given your love to, your adoring hands
Touch his so intimately that each understands,
I know, most hidden things; and when I know
Your holiest dreams yield to the stupid bow
Of his red lips, and that the empty grace
Of those strong legs and arms, that rosy face,
Has beaten your heart to such a flame of love,
That you have given him every touch and move,
Wrinkle and secret of you, all your life,
—Oh! then I know I'm waiting, lover-wife,
For the great time when love is at a close,
And all its fruit's to watch the thickening nose
And sweaty neck and dulling face and eye,
That are yours, and you, most surely, till you die!
Day after day you'll sit with him and note
The greasier tic, the dingy wrinkling coat;
As prettiness turns to pomp, and strength to fat,
And love, love, love to habit!
                                        And after that,
When all that's fine in man is at an end,
And you, that loved young life and clean, must tend

Continued on next page

A foul sick fumbling dribbling body and old,
When his rare lips hang flabby and can't hold
Slobber, and you're enduring that worst thing,
Senility's queasy furtive love-making,
And searching those dear eyes for human meaning,
Propping the bald and helpless head, and cleaning
A scrap that life's flung by, and love's forgotten—
Then you'll be tired; and passion dead and rotten;
And he'll be dirty, dirty!
                    O lithe and free
And lightfoot, that the poor heart cries to see,
That's how I'll see your man and you!—
                    But you
—Oh, when THAT time comes, you'll be dirty too!

Questions

1 How does Brooke's use of rhyme and lines that do not end at the break work to establish a certain mood and tone within this poem?

2 What is the speaker of this poem anticipating eagerly? ("Oh! then I know I'm waiting, lover-wife"). What does he fail to consider in the poem?

3 Do you think the speaker demonstrates a very mature understanding of love?

I can wade Grief

E M I L Y   D I C K I N S O N

I can wade Grief—
Whole Pools of it—
I'm used to that—
But the least push of Joy
Breaks up my feet—
And I tip—drunken—
Let no Pebble—smile—
'Twas the New Liquor—
That was all!

Power is only Pain—
Stranded, thro' Discipline,
Till Weights—will hang—
Give Balm—to Giants—
And they'll wilt, like Men—
Give Himmaleh—
They'll Carry—Him!

Questions

I can wade Grief

1 Comment on the form of this poem. Why do you think Dickinson ends almost every line with a dash?

2 According to the speaker, what effect does happiness have on her ability to cope with grief?

3 "Himmaleh" is a word that appears in another of Dickinson's poems, "The Himmaleh was known to stoop." Explain her allusion to this. What is the Himmaleh?

Ode on Melancholy

JOHN KEATS

No, no, go not to Lethe, neither twist
Wolf's-bane, tight-rooted, for its poisonous wine;
Nor suffer thy pale forehead to be kiss'd
By nightshade, ruby grape of Proserpine;
Make not your rosary of yew-berries,
Nor let the beetle, nor the death-moth be
Your mournful Psyche, nor the downy owl
A partner in your sorrow's mysteries;
For shade to shade will come too drowsily,
And drown the wakeful anguish of the soul.

But when the melancholy fit shall fall
Sudden from heaven like a weeping cloud,
That fosters the droop-headed flowers all,
And hides the green hill in an April shroud;
Then glut thy sorrow on a morning rose,
Or on the rainbow of the salt sand-wave,
Or on the wealth of globed peonies;
Or if thy mistress some rich anger shows,
Imprison her soft hand, and let her rave,
And feed deep, deep upon her peerless eyes.

She dwells with Beauty—Beauty that must die;
And Joy, whose hand is ever at his lips
Bidding adieu; and aching Pleasure nigh,
Turning to poison while the bee-mouth sips:
Ay, in the very temple of Delight
Veil'd Melancholy has her sovereign shrine,
Though seen of none save him whose strenuous tongue
Can burst Joy's grape against his palate fine;
His soul shall taste the sadness of her might,
And be among her cloudy trophies hung.

Ode on Melancholy

1 The first stanza offers advice to someone suffering from melancholy, listing things the sufferer should not do; it includes an allusion to Lethe, from Greek mythology. Why would the speaker advise the sufferer not to go there? Explain some of the other allusions in the poem.

2 How does Keats progress philosophically through the stanzas?

3 What point, ultimately, is Keats making about melancholy?

Song

ADRIENNE RICH

You're wondering if I'm lonely:
OK then, yes, I'm lonely
as a plane rides lonely and level
on its radio beam, aiming
across the Rockies
for the blue-strung aisles
of an airfield on the ocean

You want to ask, am I lonely?
Well, of course, lonely
as a woman driving across country
day after day, leaving behind
mile after mile
little towns she might have stopped
and lived and died in, lonely

If I'm lonely
it must be the loneliness
of waking first, of breathing
dawn's first cold breath on the city
of being the one awake
in a house wrapped in sleep

If I'm lonely
it's with the rowboat ice-fast on the shore
in the last red light of the year
that knows what it is, that knows it's neither
ice nor mud nor winter light
but wood, with a gift for burning

Questions Song

1. Why do you think Rich named this poem "Song" instead of, for example, "Loneliness"? What effect does the title have on the poem's contents? What does it suggest about loneliness?

2. Would you say that the speaker of this poem enjoys her solitude or longs for company? Why? How are the stanzas related?

3. Consider the image Rich leaves us with in the picture of the "rowboat ice-fast on the shore." How is it different from those in earlier sections? How does it set the final tone of the poem?

DISCOVERING GENRE:

Poetry

Family

Scar

AMY LEMMON

How delicately it runs down
your sternum, this seam paler
than your pale skin, sign
that something within has
been repaired and healed over.

After they cut you open and sewed
you back together, I longed to hold you
but could only stroke your head,
cradle your hand. Your eyelids fluttered,
your face reddened in a scream silenced
by the tube pressed against your vocal cords.

"She's crying," the nurse told us. Your voice,
softer than most infants' to begin with,
was lost until you coughed up the tube
and they had to take it out, breaking
post-op protocol. I must be heard,
and so you were, returning from
the anesthetic haze, dazed by pain

Continued on next page

and morphine for the pain. Next morning,
the woman who shuffles in to take your x-ray
hums, not gospel or "Amazing Grace,"
but "Que Sera, Sera"—a mother telling
her child What will be, will be—not quite
All's well, but close. Your cries get stronger, louder,
I beg another morphine shot for you.

Third day, I can nurse again, mindful
of your mended-china ribcage. Tears
come with the milk, and these liquids
are all I have to give, O daughter,
tiny warrior, silver-scar-bearer,
nothing at all wrong with your great heart.

Questions

Scar

1 Describe the progression of this poem, both in time and in subject.

2 "[T]hese liquids/are all I have to give" is perhaps the most important line in the poem. How does it sum up what comes before it and capture the essence of the poem in so few words? One liquid represents breastfeeding; what is the other liquid?

3 What effect does the "great" of the last line have? How would the poem differ if Lemmon had simply written, "nothing at all wrong with your heart"?

4 What three metaphors are used in this poem?

Those Winter Sundays

ROBERT HAYDEN

Sundays too my father got up early
and put his clothes on in the blueblack cold,
then with cracked hands that ached
from labor in the weekday weather made
banked fires blaze. No one ever thanked him.

I'd wake and hear the cold splintering, breaking.
When the rooms were warm, he'd call,
and slowly I would rise and dress,
fearing the chronic angers of that house,

Speaking indifferently to him,
who had driven out the cold
and polished my good shoes as well.
What did I know, what did I know
of love's austere and lonely offices?

Those Winter Sundays

1 This poem would simply be a sweet anecdote, a song of praise for the poet's father, if it weren't for hints that things aren't always perfect in the home ("fearing the chronic angers", "Speaking indifferently", "austere and lonely"). How do these hints complicate the poem, turning what was sweet into something bittersweet, even tragic?

2 What is significant about the fact that "Sundays too" the speaker's father gets up earlier than the rest of the family and takes care of warming the home?

3 Comment on the sound and literary devices Hayden uses. How do they affect the poem's tone and complement its subject matter? (For example, consonance in the first stanza mimics the sound of "the cold splintering, breaking").

Piano

D . H . L A W R E N C E

Softly, in the dusk, a woman is singing to me;
Taking me back down the vista of years, till I see
A child sitting under the piano, in the boom of the tingling strings
And pressing the small, poised feet of a mother who smiles as she sings.

In spite of myself, the insidious mastery of song
Betrays me back, till the heart of me weeps to belong
To the old Sunday evenings at home, with winter outside
And hymns in the cozy parlor, the tinkling piano our guide.

So now it is vain for the singer to burst into clamor
With the great black piano appassionato. The glamour
Of childhood days is upon me, my manhood is cast
Down in the flood of remembrance, I weep like a child for the past.

Piano

1 Compare this poem, in which the speaker reminisces about Sunday evenings with his mother, to the prior poem by Hayden, which revisits Sunday mornings with a father. Which poem, do you feel, is more loving and wistful? Which is more genuine? Which has more depth? Why?

2 A different image is born in each of the three stanzas in this poem. Describe each and, in doing so, describe the progression of the poem as it parallels the memory of the speaker.

3 While this poem rhymes, it is not in regular meter; some lines (such as the last one in the first stanza) have more feet in them than others. As a reader, how does this strike your ear? Does the verse seem awkward—do you wish for more regular meter—or do the departures from the norm add to the poem's charm?

Morning Song

SYLVIA PLATH

Love set you going like a fat gold watch.
The midwife slapped your footsoles, and your bald cry
Took its place among the elements.

Our voices echo, magnifying your arrival. New statue.
In a drafty museum, your nakedness
Shadows our safety. We stand round blankly as walls.

I'm no more your mother
Than the cloud that distills a mirror to reflect its own slow
Effacement at the wind's hand.

All night your moth-breath
Flickers among the flat pink roses. I wake to listen:
A far sea moves in my ear.

One cry, and I stumble from bed, cow-heavy and floral
In my Victorian nightgown.
Your mouth opens clean as a cat's. The window square

Whitens and swallows its dull stars. And now you try
Your handful of notes;
The clear vowels rise like balloons.

Morning Song

1 "Morning Song" depicts new motherhood both as something animal ("cow heavy"; "clean as a cat's"; "moth-breath") and as something that creates distance and is foreign, almost alien ("far sea," "New statue / In a drafty museum"; "I'm no more your mother"). How does this create tension in the poem? Which of the views (if either) is dominant by the poem's end?

2 Explain the analogy made between the cloud and the mother.

3 The poem, although harsh at times, ends on a relatively quiet note. What effect does this create? How would the tone of the poem change if, for example, Plath had moved the third stanza and the last line of the poem ended with "cat"?

I Go Back to May 1937

Sharon Olds

I see them standing at the formal gates of their colleges,
I see my father strolling out
under the ochre sandstone arch, the
red tiles glinting like bent
plates of blood behind his head, I
see my mother with a few light books at her hip
standing at the pillar made of tiny bricks with the
wrought-iron gate still open behind her, its
sword-tips back in the May air,
they are about to graduate, they are about to get married,
they are kids, they are dumb, all they know is they are
innocent, they would never hurt anybody.
I want to go up to them and say Stop,
don't do it—she's the wrong woman,
he's the wrong man, you are going to do things
you cannot imagine you would ever do,
you are going to do bad things to children,
you are going to suffer in ways you never heard of,
you are going to want to die. I want to go
up to them there in the May sunlight and say it,
her hungry pretty blank face turning to me,
her pitiful beautiful untouched body,
his arrogant handsome blind face turning to me,
his pitiful beautiful untouched body,
but I don't do it. I want to live. I
take them up like male and female
paper dolls and bang then together
at the hips like chips of flint as if to
strike sparks from them, I say
Do what you are going to do, and I will tell about it.

Questions
I Go Back to May 1937

1 Consider the way repetition, anaphora, and parallelism work in Olds' poem. How do they lend an urgent, song-like quality and feel to "I Go Back to May 1937"?

2 How does the poem's closing line comment on the existence of the poem?

3 What statement is the speaker making about hindsight and knowledge when she writes "but I don't do it. I want to live"?

4 What are some of the literary techniques the author uses in the poem, other than those mentioned in the first question?

Work Ethics

E M I L Y L L O Y D

My father is kicking my mother out on a school night
and I have to be Jackson Pollock tomorrow morning
in seventh grade. All day, I've tried to brood
in the mirror in my father's shirt, to hang
a cigarette from my lip and keep it there
throughout my speech.
     She's having an affair—
a keeper. In a week the man will walk
off to buy us sodas and she'll stick
an elbow in me, saying *Isn't he cute?*

The cigarette is fake: a piece of chalk;
I've marked the end with orange to mimic ash.
I'm scared to death of what I'll have to say
tomorrow, now I've decided to tell the story
of someone asking Pollock How do you know
when you're done with a painting? Jackson, calmly, softly:
How do you know when you're finished making love?
Falling dresses. My mother's: my father's
sobbing, dropping them from a second story

window. I'm not sure I can say make love
in front of friends. I will. I'll say, Sure Mom,
he's cute. A falling dress half-floats,
half-thuds. Do you know when you're finished making love?
It's a school night, there's work to be done, the cigarette
falls and rolls across the family room
and nothing burns.

Questions **Work Ethics**

1 Why do you think Lloyd titled this poem "Work Ethics"? What "work" is being done?

2 Poetry is, for the most part, economical: every phrase, detail, or image is there for a reason. Given that, what do you make of the detail that the speaker is looking in the mirror, while wearing her "father's shirt"?

3 This poem is written in "loose" verse, with no apparent structure or rhyme scheme. It appears to follow the poet's train of thought. Identify places in the poem that support this theory.

My Papa's Waltz

THEODORE ROETHKE

The whiskey on your breath
Could make a small boy dizzy;
But I hung on like death:
Such waltzing was not easy.

We romped until the pans
Slid from the kitchen shelf;
My mother's countenance
Could not unfrown itself.

The hand that held my wrist
Was battered on one knuckle;
At every step you missed
My right ear scraped a buckle.

You beat time on my head
With a palm caked hard by dirt,
Then waltzed me off to bed
Still clinging to your shirt.

Questions

My Papa's Waltz

1. Readers who lived when Roethke wrote this poem (1948) and the generation to follow have read it as a fairly light and fond remembrance of a father who, while a bit rough from his working day, finds time to dance with his son before putting him to bed. Interestingly, however, some more modern readers have read it as a description of abuse. Which interpretation feels right to you? Why?

2. "My Papa's Waltz" is written in iambic trimeter. While iambic pentameter has five feet per line, iambic trimeter has three feet per line. Why is this meter appropriate for a poem about a waltz? What about the rhyme sequence?

3. The central symbol of this poem is a waltz. In line four, the speaker states that "such waltzing was not easy," although the waltz is not, traditionally, a complicated dance. What do you think is meant, then, by the speaker's assertion? Do you see the waltz as a positive or a negative symbol?

My Father's Love Letters

YUSEF KOMUNYAKAA

On Fridays he'd open a can of Jax
After coming home from the mill,
& ask me to write a letter to my mother
Who sent postcards of desert flowers
Taller than men. He would beg,
Promising to never beat her
Again. Somehow I was happy
She had gone, & sometimes wanted
To slip in a reminder, how Mary Lou
Williams' "Polka Dots & Moonbeams"
Never made the swelling go down.
His carpenter's apron always bulged
With old nails, a claw hammer
Looped at his side & extension cords
Coiled around his feet.
Words rolled from under the pressure
Of my ballpoint: Love,
Baby, Honey, Please.
We sat in the quiet brutality
Of voltage meters & pipe threaders,
Lost between sentences…
The gleam of a five-pound wedge
On the concrete floor
Pulled a sunset
Through the doorway of his toolshed.
I wondered if she laughed
& held them over a gas burner.
My father could only sign

His name, but he'd look at blueprints
& say how many bricks
Formed each wall. This man,
Who stole roses & hyacinth
For his yard, would stand there
With eyes closed & fists balled,
Laboring over a simple word, almost
Redeemed by what he tried to say.

My Father's Love Letters

Questions

1 What are some of the contrasts found in the poem? What information is not stated directly?

2 With whom do your sympathies lie in this poem?

3 What is the irony in the title, "My Father's Love Letters"?

Pear

E D U A R D O   C .   C O R R A L

Middle child, conqueror
of tree houses, my brother bites a pear,
the bite mark casts a pale light

that illuminates the story book on his desk.
His favorite illustration: children
playing tug-of-war

beneath the sprawling branches of an oak.
Boys versus girls. He runs
his thumb over the face

of the tallest girl, her socks
embroidered with yellow rosettes.
He bites the pear again, the light increases,

enough for him to notice,
for the first time, the silver cross
around the girl's neck.

If mother reads to him from the book
he begs her to pronounce
the name of the girl. She insists

Continued on next page

her name isn't mentioned in the story.
So he's taken the jangling
of mother's copper bangles as she turns

the pages for her name.
He adores the girl's intense grip
on the rope. He can't read. Not yet.

He glances at his hands,
and though holding a pear,
feels rope sliding between his palms.

Questions Pear

1 What is the significance of the pear?

2 "Pear" concerns a kind of learning, a kind of awakening. Certain words Corral uses hint at the speaker's brother's growing awareness. Jot down the words (verbs, adjectives, nouns) that seem to carry the most suggestive weight. What kind of awakening does the poem describe?

3 The subject of the poem is the "middle child." Do you think the speaker is an older or younger sibling? What details help you form an opinion?

4 Corral makes use of lines that connect each unrhymed tercet. For example, the first stanza ends with "the bite mark casts a pale light," while the second begins with "that illuminates the story book on his desk." Why do you think Corral chose to structure his poem in this manner?

Two Fish Stories

STEVEN D. SCHROEDER

With pileworm bait, Grandpa and I
dropped lines off San Francisco docks
when I was four, once almost caught
two seaperch on a single hook,
one a tail clinging to the other
in hunger or denial, stunted
sawteeth unwilling to let go
until pier-level, when it splashed
back in the bay, its flashy scales
shivering as it fled to live
a little. Twenty-two years later,
at his retirement home—no, cottage—
after I fished the Colorado,
we talked about the "ugly-bugs"
he'd tied, brown hair and hackle twisted
on flies he snelled because of eyes
too focused elsewhere to thread line;
about my only catch, "green trout,"
algae the hot spring sulfur spawns
and sends in streamers down the river;
about no more. His birthday loomed
three weeks away, a last long cast
reeled slowly to the shore. Unhooked
but grasping, tugged two ways, I shook
his hand before we both let go.

Questions · Two Fish Stories

1 Consider the title. What is the meaning of a "fish story"? What are the "two" fish stories Schroeder tells?

2 How are the fish stories revealed as a metaphor in the final five lines of the poem?

3 "Two Fish Stories" is composed of four sentences stretched over twenty-five lines. How do Schroeder's longer, multi-clause sentences affect your reading and the pacing of this poem?

My Grandmother's Love Letters

HART CRANE

There are no stars to-night
But those of memory.
Yet how much room for memory there is
In the loose girdle of soft rain.

There is even room enough
For the letters of my mother's mother,
Elizabeth,
That have been pressed so long
Into a corner of the roof
That they are brown and soft,
And liable to melt as snow.

Over the greatness of such space
Steps must be gentle.
It is all hung by an invisible white hair.
It trembles as birch limbs webbing the air.

And I ask myself:

"Are your fingers long enough to play
Old keys that are but echoes:
Is the silence strong enough
To carry back the music to its source
And back to you again
As though to her?"

Yet I would lead my grandmother by the hand
Through much of what she would not understand;
And so I stumble. And the rain continues on the roof
With such a sound of gently pitying laughter.

Questions
My Grandmother's Love Letters

1 Compare this poem to "Piano" by D.H. Lawrence, which appears earlier in this section. Which do you find more effective? Why?

2 Crane's poem is in free verse, but he occasionally employs end-rhyme ("white hair/the air" "hand/understand"). How does this moving in and out of rhyme echo the action of the poem?

3 In the first half of this poem (the first two stanzas), the speaker discusses finding his grandmother's love letters and feeling a desire to communicate with her. How does the poem shift in its second half when the speaker asks himself: "Are your fingers long enough to play / Old keys that are but echoes"?

Madeline Island

TERESA BALLARD

She is studying the place where flies
have gathered to lay their eggs,
investigating life with the point of her stick.
One small flick and the universe is over.
The trout returns to the pond belly up,
floats, turns, and is now a boat
to be guided by six-year-old currents.
When done she'll gather flat stones from the shore,
bury then unbury the dead, look for signs
of movement or change. It doesn't matter
that everything is dying. Last week
two wings beat in her hand, then stopped.
She doesn't know that the song of her body
will straighten. All around her
the world is open like a cut.

Questions
Madeline Island

1 Explain how the manner in which 'Madeline Island" is written serves to distance the speaker (and thus the reader) from the subject she observes.

2 "Madelinc Island" is part a lament, part a celebration—a portrait of a child's innocence and curiosity. While the speaker describes the girl, we learn almost as much about her. Describe the speaker.

3 The poem's last word, "cut," bears a great weight. We are familiar with viewing the world or future as an open door or open field; the world as an open cut, though, is a jarring image. Explain how it impacts the tone of the poem.

4 Explain the title.

DISCOVERING GENRE:

Poetry

Love

The Sun Rising

JOHN DONNE

Busy old fool, unruly Sun,
Why dost thou thus,
Through windows, and through curtains, call on us?
Must to thy motions lovers' seasons run?
Saucy pedantic wretch, go chide
Late school-boys and sour prentices,
Go tell court-huntsmen that the king will ride,
Call country ants to harvest offices;
Love, all alike, no season knows nor clime,
Nor hours, days, months, which are the rags of time.

Thy beams so reverend, and strong
Why shouldst thou think?
I could eclipse and cloud them with a wink,
But that I would not lose her sight so long.
If her eyes have not blinded thine,
Look, and to-morrow late tell me,
Whether both th' Indias of spice and mine
Be where thou left'st them, or lie here with me.
Ask for those kings whom thou saw'st yesterday,
And thou shalt hear, "All here in one bed lay."

Continued on next page

She's all states, and all princes I;
Nothing else is.
Princes do but play us; compared to this,
All honour's mimic, all wealth alchemy.
Thou, Sun, art half as happy as we,
In that the world's contracted thus;
Thine age asks ease, and since thy duties be
To warm the world, that's done in warming us.
Shine here to us, and thou art everywhere;
This bed thy center is, these walls thy sphere.

Questions

The Sun Rising

1 In lines like "Thy beams so reverend, and strong / Why shouldst thou think," Donne's speaker addresses the sun in much the same way the speaker addresses Death in "Holy Sonnet X." Look at that poem in the Death and Loss section of this book. Compare and contrast the styles and tones of the two speakers.

2 "The Sun Rising" is a particular kind of a love poem, called an aubade. Aubades are songs or poems about lovers being parted in the morning, and here we find Donne's speaker blaming the sun for ending his time with his beloved. He tells the sun to attend to other duties, like waking those late for work, because love "no season knows"—no hour of the day, or time of year, has more meaning than any other when one is in love. Finally, though, rather than attend to other duties, the speaker invites the sun to stay there and warm the lovers, because they themselves are the whole world. What do you make of this shift in commands?

3 Hyperbole is exaggeration for effect, and Donne puts it to extreme use in "The Sun Rising." What hyperbolic assertions does Donne center his poem around? What is the effect of these assertions upon the meaning of the poem?

Sonnets from the Portuguese: XIV

ELIZABETH BARRETT BROWNING

If thou must love me, let it be for naught
Except for love's sake only. Do not say
"I love her for her smile—her look—her way
Of speaking gently,—for a trick of thought
That falls in well with mine, and certes brought
A sense of pleasant ease on such a day"—
For these things in themselves, Beloved, may
Be changed, or change for thee,—and love, so wrought,
May be unwrought so. Neither love me for
Thine own dear pity's wiping my cheeks dry,—
A creature might forget to weep, who bore
Thy comfort long, and lose thy love thereby!
But love me for love's sake, that evermore
Thou mayst love on, through love's eternity.

Questions

Sonnetts from the Portuguese: XIV

1 The speaker passionately asks to be loved "for love's sake only"—not for any physical characteristics she possesses, not even for her personality. All of these things may change, she says. It's an interesting argument and request. How does one love "for love's sake only"? Comment on the ideas Browning raises in her poem.

2 What effect do the sonnet's regular rhyme scheme and meter have on this poem? Is this an example of a Petrarchan or Shakespearean sonnet?

3 In Shakespeare's *Romeo and Juliet,* Juliet cautions Romeo,

> "O, swear not by the moon, the inconstant moon,
> That monthly changes in her circled orb,
> Lest that thy love prove likewise variable."

Compare her request to Browning's lines:

> "For these things in themselves, Beloved, may
> Be changed, or change for thee,—and love, so wrought,
> May be unwrought so."

How are the thoughts expressed by Shakespeare and Browning similar?

Sonnet CXXX

WILLIAM SHAKESPEARE

My mistress' eyes are nothing like the sun;
Coral is far more red than her lips' red;
If snow be white, why then her breasts are dun;
If hairs be wires, black wires grow on her head.
I have seen roses damasked, red and white,
But no such roses see I in her cheeks;
And in some perfumes is there more delight
Than in the breath that from my mistress reeks.
I love to hear her speak, yet well I know
That music hath a far more pleasing sound;
I grant I never saw a goddess go;
My mistress when she walks treads on the ground.
And yet, by heaven, I think my love as rare
As any she belied with false compare.

Questions
Sonnett CXXX

1 With this sonnet, Shakespeare is indirectly criticizing love poetry's tradition of exaggerating the beloved's traits—saying her breath is like perfume or her eyes are like stars, for example. The first twelve lines read almost like insults. For example, the fact that he cannot see any flowers in her cheeks is, of course, unflattering to the speaker's "mistress." But Shakespearean sonnets are structured so that the last two lines turn away from the previous lines, sometimes including a twist and sometimes merely stating a change in the speaker's tone or outlook. How does this sonnet's concluding couplet change the meaning of the lines that came before it?

2 Elizabeth Barrett Browning's "Sonnets from the Portuguese: XIV" is a Petrarchan sonnet. Both Shakespearean sonnets and Petrarchan sonnets contain fourteen lines, but the rhyme schemes are quite different. Revisit Browning's sonnet and compare its rhyme scheme and subject to those of this sonnet by Shakespeare.

3 Explore the various comparisons Shakespeare uses. How does he glorify and praise his love through the use of insults?

"Should the wide world roll away"

STEPHEN CRANE

Should the wide world roll away,
Leaving black terror,
Limitless night,
Nor God, nor man, nor place to stand
Would be to me essential,
If thou and thy white arms were there,
And the fall to doom a long way.

Questions

"Should the wide world roll away"

1 Crane's free verse poem includes such a twist in its final lines, which is a technique used in sonnets as well. Explain the turn in his thought.

2 Look at the last line. How does it change the impact of the next-to-last line? How would the poem be different, and the poet's statement about love different, if it ended with "and thy white arms were there"?

3 Consider Crane's use of such phrases as "wide world," "black terror," "limitless night," and "white arms." How would you describe the language, rhythm, rhyme, and use of words in the poem? Is it effective or not? Explain.

XO

P A U L   G U E S T

If aliens in invisible orbit intercepted
my love letters to you, at the end
of each they might think, *he's through,*
thank God, assuming, of course,
He's reached them. Even light,
the alpha and omega of all
speed, cannot help but be forever
tardy. They might think
of each paltry code our kind has made,
SOS, semaphore, Braille
raised like a rash, and the code
of which we're made, in our cells
interlaced. XO ending
so many of the notes,
they might think I speak of football,
that I have begun to diagram the rudiments
of our game plan, the one that will rocket us back
from loss. Maybe they are curious
why these sounds
above the two dozen others in our mouths
mean how I would touch you
and why RQ does not in the slightest mean
all day I have ached for just your ear
or why UL does not abbreviate
the breath I've spent trying not to say your name
and maybe they do not care
and in their chill orbits

their own love letters beam back through dark vacuum
what they have learned
and how savage this world is
and the food is not like home
and the bed is a garden seeded with lumps
and write soon
and though it is no substitute
let us believe that this is my hug and this is my kiss.

Questions XO

1 Describe the subject and situation of this poem. How is the subject portrayed?

2 How would you describe the central idea or theme Guest is trying to convey? Why did he use aliens as the method of getting his concept of love across?

3 How do the final three lines bring the reader back to the lovers' reality?

Poem for a 75th Birthday

MARILYN L. TAYLOR

Love of my life, it's nearly evening
and here you still are, slow-dancing
in your garden, folding and unfolding
like an enormous grasshopper in the waning
sun. Somehow you've turned our rectangle
of clammy clay into Southern California,
where lilacs and morning-glories mingle
with larkspur, ladyfern and zinnia—
all of them a little drunk on thundershowers
and the broth of newly fallen flowers.

I can't get over how the brightest blooms
seem to come reaching for your hand,
weaving their way across the loom
of your fingers, bending
toward the trellis of your body.
They sway on their skinny stems
like a gang of super-models
making fabulous displays of their dumb
and utter gratitude, as if they knew
they'd be birdseed if it weren't for you.

Continued on next page

And yet they haven't got the slightest clue
about the future; they behave as if
you'll be there for them always, as if you
were the sun itself, brilliant enough
to keep them in the pink, or gold, or green
forever. Understandable, I decide
as I look at you out there—as I lean
in your direction, absolutely satisfied
that summer afternoon is all
there is, and night will never fall.

Poem for a 75th Birthday

1 What comparison does Taylor draw between the garden's flowers and the speaker?

2 Describe the form of the poem. How does Taylor choose to divide her stanzas?

3 What is the central idea the poet is trying to convey?

Song: Mediocrity in Love Rejected

THOMAS CAREW

Give me more love, or more disdain;
The torrid or the frozen zone
Bring equal ease unto my pain,
The temperate affords me none;
Either extreme, of love or hate,
Is sweeter than a calm estate.

Give me a storm; if it be love,
Like Danae in that golden shower,
I swim in pleasure; if it prove
Disdain, that torrent will devour
My vulture hopes; and he's possessed
Of heaven, that's but from hell released.
Then crown my joys, or cure my pain;
Give me more love, or more disdain.

Questions

Song: Mediocrity in Love Rejected

1 Like Barrett Browning's speaker in "Sonnets from the Portuguese: XIV," Carew's speaker commands that his beloved love him in a certain way. Descriptions of how one wants to be loved are common in love poetry. Why do you think Carew's speaker would prefer outright disdain to a "mediocre" or not-fully-passionate form of love? What does his request suggest is most painful in a romantic relationship?

2 Is Carew's poem a sonnet? Why or why not?

3 Carew uses opposites, such as love and disdain, hot and cold, and ease and pain throughout his first stanza. Why do you think Carew juxtaposes these things?

Her Lips
Are Copper Wire

JEAN TOOMER

whisper of yellow globes
gleaming on lamp-posts that sway
like bootleg licker drinkers in the fog

and let your breath be moist against me
like bright beads on yellow globes

telephone the power-house
that the main wires are insulate

(her words play softly up and down
dewy corridors of billboards)

then with your tongue remove the tape
and press your lips to mine
till they are incandescent

Her Lips Are Copper Wire

1 Comment on the electrical imagery in the poem, which is a more modern one than most of the love poems here. What comparison is being made?

2 What do you make of the shift between "her" and "your" in this poem? Who is speaking, and who is being addressed?

3 Find some instances of sound devices and literary terms in the poem. How does Toomer's use of sound affect the poem's tone?

I Shall Forget You Presently, My Dear

Edna St. Vincent Millay

I shall forget you presently, my dear,
So make the most of this, your little day,
Your little month, your little half a year,
Ere I forget, or die, or move away,
And we are done forever; by and by
I shall forget you, as I said, but now,
If you entreat me with your loveliest lie
I will protest you with my favorite vow.
I would indeed that love were longer-lived,
And oaths were not so brittle as they are,
But so it is, and nature has contrived
To struggle on without a break thus far,—
Whether or not we find what we are seeking
Is idle, biologically speaking.

I Shall Forget You
Presently, My Dear

1 Comment on the form of the poem. What type of poem is it, and what qualities make it so?

2 How does Millay's subject shift within the sonnet?

3 What do you think Millay meant by her final couplet, "Whether or not we find what we are seeking / Is idle, biologically speaking"?

Deciding on Quandary

AMY LEMMON

"Hug" is a word too pink and squat
to mean four arms taking their places,
as we let bold gravity use those limbs
to fill in our hungriest spaces.

But "embrace," with its elegant Latin roots,
seems brittle and forced, like jewels
sewn thick on a light cotton T-shirt,
when they'd rather adorn sleek formals.

And "holding" implies something lifted up,
although "holding on" is closer—
as if the cling of shoulder and chin
kept us from dropping to danger.

Like the spin it describes, "quandary"
has left us no clues to its origin,
so I'll use it to sound like the tangle
we tried not, but needed, to fall in.

P R E S T W I C K   H O U S E

Deciding on Quandary

1 What is the poet's "quandary"? What is finally decided upon as a solution to this problem?

2 Discuss the structure and rhyme scheme of this poem. What literary devices are used? How do these things affect the tone of the poem?

3 Discuss the poet's use of imagery and its effect upon the poem. Consider such phrases as "pink and squat" to describe a hug, and "like jewels / sewn thick on a light cotton T-shirt" to describe an embrace. How do the images impact the message of the poem?

To His Coy Mistress

ANDREW MARVELL

Had we but world enough, and time,
This coyness, lady, were no crime.
We would sit down and think which way
To walk, and pass our long love's day;
Thou by the Indian Ganges' side
Shouldst rubies find; I by the tide
Of Humber would complain. I would
Love you ten years before the Flood;
And you should, if you please, refuse
Till the conversion of the Jews.
My vegetable love should grow
Vaster than empires, and more slow.
An hundred years should go to praise
Thine eyes, and on thy forehead gaze;
Two hundred to adore each breast,
But thirty thousand to the rest;
An age at least to every part,
And the last age should show your heart.
For, lady, you deserve this state,
Nor would I love at lower rate.

But at my back I always hear
Time's winged chariot hurrying near;
And yonder all before us lie
Deserts of vast eternity.
Thy beauty shall no more be found,
Nor, in thy marble vault, shall sound
My echoing song; then worms shall try
That long preserv'd virginity,
And your quaint honour turn to dust,
And into ashes all my lust.
The grave's a fine and private place,
But none I think do there embrace.

Now therefore, while the youthful hue
Sits on thy skin like morning dew,
And while thy willing soul transpires
At every pore with instant fires,
Now let us sport us while we may;
And now, like am'rous birds of prey,
Rather at once our time devour,
Than languish in his slow-chapp'd power.
Let us roll all our strength, and all
Our sweetness, up into one ball;
And tear our pleasures with rough strife
Thorough the iron gates of life.
Thus, though we cannot make our sun
Stand still, yet we will make him run.

To His Coy Mistress

1 "To His Coy Mistress" is written in well-defined iambic tetrameter—i.e., eight iambic feet per line. Despite the meter continuing regularly in this vein throughout the poem, though, the tempo speeds up noticeably by the third stanza. Why do you think this is the case? How does the concept of time's passing work in the poem?

2 The poem undergoes a shift in tone as well as structure as it progresses. Discuss the tone as you perceive it in each stanza.

3 How is this poem an exercise in irony?

Euphonic Sounds

J A M E S   G U R L E Y

"What's scurrilously called ragtime's
an invention here to stay."
       –Scott Joplin
       –Sedalia, MO, 1899

In the gas chandeliers' sway,
tobacco smoke swirls and syncopated chords
from an upright piano, Joplin
presides over drunken cakewalking,
buck and wing steppers who heed the call
of his latest rag, a tune part song,
part breath. In the July heat of this night,
this century turning Joplin's rag
celebrates a new signature.
The piano almost a march, the blues played
in some lover's embrace, a losing hand.
The blues into the fourth chorus,
says: *O this suffering, these weary bones—*
as the piano grabs hold of the body,
tells everything that will happen to it:
I still love you, you hurt me.
The same exhaustion of ravers, break-dancers
under a neon kaleidoscope in a haze

Continued on next page

where what they touch pulsates,
where a rapper in baggy pants and jacket
spins out tales of bravado, want—
the rhymes' power, his words'
staccato becomes our own catharsis.
The blues in the bloodstream,
as it was for Joplin once at the Maple Leaf,
caught in a late-night jubilee—
the hunger's hard work consuming us:
O Forgive me, please love, Hold me.
That refrain, until there's no way
for our body not to surrender.
Prairie breezes from an open window singing
the rag, its blessed cool relief,
as Joplin resolves the tune's dissonance
in sweet measures, riffs, the dancers
falling only to rise astounded, to shake
these blues loose. Our abandon
downright scandalous.

Questions

Euphonic Sounds

1 Study Gurley's line composition. What technique do you notice? Keeping in mind that such things are deliberate, why do you think Gurley chose to compose his lines in this manner?

2 How does Gurley forge a link between the beginning years of the twentieth century and more modern times?

3 Which time period does the speaker, not necessarily the poet, prefer. In which one is he living?

Delight in Disorder

ROBERT HERRICK

A sweet disorder in the dress
Kindles in clothes a wantonness.
A lawn about the shoulders thrown
Into a fair distraction;
An erring lace which here and there
Enthralls the crimson stomacher;
A cuff neglectful, and thereby
Ribbons to flow confusedly;
A winning wave, deserving note,
In the tempestuous petticoat;
A careless shoestring, in whose tie
I see a wild civility;
Do more bewitch me than when art
Is too precise in every part.

Delight in Disorder

1 What is the effect of the poet's choosing to use "art" to describe a certain manner of dressing? What impact does this choice have on the overall tone of the poem?

2 Fashion and careful dress are part of culture and "civility." The opposite of civil society is the natural world. Which words in "Delight in Disorder" evoke the natural world?

3 What is the general tone of the poem?

DISCOVERING GENRE:

Poetry

Self-Knowledge

After Apple-Picking

R O B E R T   F R O S T

My long two-pointed ladder's sticking through a tree
Toward heaven still,
And there's a barrel that I didn't fill
Beside it, and there may be two or three
Apples I didn't pick upon some bough.
But I am done with apple-picking now.
Essence of winter sleep is on the night,
The scent of apples: I am drowsing off.
I cannot rub the strangeness from my sight
I got from looking through a pane of glass
I skimmed this morning from the drinking trough
And held against the world of hoary grass.
It melted, and I let it fall and break.
But I was well
Upon my way to sleep before it fell,
And I could tell
What form my dreaming was about to take.
Magnified apples appear and disappear,
Stem end and blossom end,
And every fleck of russet showing clear.
My instep arch not only keeps the ache,
It keeps the pressure of a ladder-round.
I feel the ladder sway as the boughs bend.
And I keep hearing from the cellar bin
The rumbling sound

Continued on next page

Of load on load of apples coming in.
For I have had too much
Of apple-picking: I am overtired
Of the great harvest I myself desired.
There were ten thousand thousand fruit to touch,
Cherish in hand, lift down, and not let fall.
For all
That struck the earth,
No matter if not bruised or spiked with stubble,
Went surely to the cider-apple heap
As of no worth.
One can see what will trouble
This sleep of mine, whatever sleep it is.
Were he not gone,
The woodchuck could say whether it's like his
Long sleep, as I describe its coming on,
Or just some human sleep.

Questions
After Apple-Picking

1 How would you describe the tone of the speaker in this poem? Is he simply weary from the work of picking apples?

2 The ideas of labor and sleep operate on both literal and figurative meanings in this poem. On a literal level, Frost refers to a hard day's labor and slumber at the end of that day. What is he speaking of on a figurative level?

3 At what point in the poem do you begin to see that the poem is not about merely picking apples? What clues does Frost give that would indicate that this poem takes place during the winter? What literary devices does he use? How does Frost employ sound and rhyme in the poem?

The Road Not Taken

ROBERT FROST

Two roads diverged in a yellow wood,
And sorry I could not travel both
And be one traveler, long I stood
And looked down one as far as I could
To where it bent in the undergrowth.

Then took the other, as just as fair,
And having perhaps the better claim,
Because it was grassy and wanted wear;
Though as for that the passing there
Had worn them really about the same.

And both that morning equally lay
In leaves no step had trodden black.
Oh, I kept the first for another day!
Yet knowing how way leads on to way,
I doubted if I should ever come back.

I shall be telling this with a sigh
Somewhere ages and ages hence:
Two roads diverged in a wood, and I—
I took the one less traveled by,
And that has made all the difference.

The Road Not Taken

1 Many people have interpreted Frost's poem as an inspirational one that encourages people to take the "road less traveled by." What clues in the poem indicate that an opposite interpretation exists, one that expresses sorrow about the choice?

2 Why do you think Frost titled this poem "The Road Not Taken" instead of "The Road Less Traveled"?

3 Frost has long been a proponent of poetry that does not necessarily need to be characterized by strict poetic form and structure. Many of his poems, such as "Mending Wall" and "Out—Out—," show this characteristic of his style. Why do you think he uses a very regular form and structure in this particular poem?

Tremor

(ON EPILEPSY)

REBECCA LOUDON

Begin here: the index finger of my right hand twitching,
bony fish attached to hand, arm, elbow, shoulder cup
and ball, the stem of neck, my brain—
that faulty toy.

Begin here: he shaves my hair. I catch blonde clumps
as they fall. He opens my skull, presses with his thumb
here, here and here, brain coil wet and pulsing
like those black and white movies where hunched men
scoop and dig.

Begin here: Saturday mornings, across the street
from my mother's house. Frances Berry carries a cup of tea,
rattle-rattle-rattles her way from the kitchen, rice-paper napkins,
Prokofiev, the smell of turpentine and linseed oil.

Begin here: my brain's slick hive disconnected from its queen,
popping in spiky green lines. *What do you see when I push here?*
A knit hat, my pink shoes, stop, stop,
oh, such a pop.

Tremor

1 What do you think is Loudon's point in starting each stanza "Begin here"? Where should one begin?

2 Comment on the following image: "brain coil wet and pulsing/ like those black and white movies where hunched men/scoop and dig." How does it suggest the speaker feels about her illness? Locate and explain some other key images.

3 How does Loudon use imagery and repetition to help convey her assessment of the speaker and the illness?

Invictus

WILLIAM ERNEST HENLEY

Out of the night that covers me,
　　Black as the Pit from pole to pole,
I thank whatever gods may be
　　For my unconquerable soul.

In the fell clutch of circumstance
　　I have not winced nor cried aloud.
Under the bludgeonings of chance
　　My head is bloody, but unbowed.

Beyond this place of wrath and tears
　　Looms but the horror of the shade,
And yet the menace of the years
　　Finds, and shall find me, unafraid.

It matters not how strait the gate,
　　How charged with punishments the scrolls,
I am the master of my fate:
　　I am the captain of my soul.

Invictus

❶ What does the speaker mean in saying, "My head is bloody, but unbowed"?

❷ Why do you think Henley began the last two lines "I am"?

❸ How is this a poem about being true to one's self?

"I'm Nobody! Who are you?"

EMILY DICKINSON

I'm Nobody! Who are you?
Are you Nobody, too?
Then there's a pair of us! Don't tell!
They'd banish us, you know!

How dreary to be somebody!
How public, like a Frog
To tell your name the livelong day
To an admiring Bog!

"I'm Nobody! Who are you?"

1 Comment on the tone of this poem. Do you find it witty or sad? Explain.

2 Why do you think the speaker is convinced that if others knew about the two "nobodies," "they" would "banish"? Who are "they"?

3 What does Dickinson use in this poem to affect the tone and meaning?

Keeping Things Whole

MARK STRAND

In a field
I am the absence
of field.
This is
always the case.
Wherever I am
I am what is missing.

When I walk
I part the air
and always
the air moves in
to fill the spaces
where my body's been.

We all have reasons
for moving.
I move
to keep things whole.

Questions
Keeping Things Whole

1 This free verse poem is written in very short lines; some contain only two words. Only one word, "Wherever," has more than two syllables. There are no literary devices used, like simile or metaphor. What is said, however, is not simplistic. How does this affect your understanding of the poem?

2 What is the essential meaning of the poem?

3 How would you describe the author's tone in this poem? What does Strand mean when he writes, "Wherever I am / I am what is missing"?

World-Strangeness

SIR WILLIAM WATSON

Strange the world about me lies,
Never yet familiar grown—
Still disturbs me with surprise,
Haunts me like a face half known.

In this house with starry dome,
Floored with gemlike plains and seas,
Shall I never feel at home,
Never wholly be at ease?

On from room to room I stray,
Yet my Host can ne'er espy,
And I know not to this day
Whether guest, or captive I.

So, betwixt the starry dome
And the floor of plains and seas,
I have never felt at home,
Never wholly been at ease.

Questions
World-Strangeness

1 In the poem's fifth line, Watson refers to the world as a "house." How does this make the later refrain about never feeling "at home" stronger?

2 The poet asks and answers a question in "World Strangeness." Why in particular does he never feel at ease? What reason does he give for his uneasiness?

3 "World-Strangeness" is composed in a regular metrical pattern of syllables and accents. What is the effect of this meter? What words and phrases contribute to the message of the poem?

Catching the Scent

A N N E   H A I N E S

Summer evenings, I was put
to bed before dark. I'd kneel
on the mattress to look out the window
and watch my mother talking
to the neighbor across the fence,
standing near the roses that bloomed
though we never took care of them.
The evening light was long and soft
falling across the lawn.
I couldn't hear my mother's voice
and she didn't turn to see me
watching. That summer
I began to see her life as separate
from mine,
       in long light, among roses.
Later, I'd wake in the dark
and lift my face into night air,
the insistent breeze of far places.
At the edge of town cars hummed
on the speedway, their sound
punctuated by the rasp of cicadas
calling to each other.
           In moonglow
and in half-sleep, I imagine
the night as an open place
stretching out around me.
I cannot see the roses
but smell them blooming
on dark wind.

Catching the Scent

1 Recall that, in poetry, random details and words are rare; for the most part, every image is placed in the poem for a reason. Given that, what do you make of the detail that cars are humming "on the speedway"? Why do you think Haines includes it?

2 What is the point of mentioning that the speaker can smell, but not see, the roses?

3 What might the author's purpose be in indenting the two lines that she does?

"I am the only being whose doom…"

EMILY BRONTË

I am the only being whose doom
No tongue would ask no eye would mourn
I never caused a thought of gloom
A smile of joy since I was born

In secret pleasure—secret tears
This changeful life has slipped away
As friendless after eighteen years
As lone as on my natal day

There have been times I cannot hide
There have been times when this was drear
When my sad soul forgot its pride
And longed for one to love me here

But those were in the early glow
Of feelings since subdued by care
And they have died so long ago
I hardly now believe they were

First melted off the hope of youth
Then Fancy's rainbow fast withdrew
And then experience told me truth
In mortal bosoms never grew

'Twas grief enough to think mankind
All hollow servile insincere—
But worse to trust to my own mind
And find the same corruption there

Questions
"I am the only being whose doom..."

1 Analyze the structure and rhyme scheme of this poem. Do you think it fits with the poem's subject?

2 How does the first line, "I am the only being whose doom," illustrate the severity of the speaker's perceived isolation? How does it establish the tone of the poem to follow?

3 What realization does the speaker make in the last stanza regarding the world's insincerity and about herself? How does this realization affect her isolation?

DISCOVERING GENRE:

Poetry

Death and Loss

"Because I could not stop for Death"

EMILY DICKINSON

Because I could not stop for Death—
He kindly stopped for me—
The Carriage held but just Ourselves—
And Immortality.

We slowly drove—He knew no haste
And I had put away
My labor and my leisure too,
For His Civility—

We passed the School, where Children
strove
At Recess—in the Ring—
We passed the fields of Gazing Grain—
We passed the Setting Sun—

Or rather—He passed Us—
The Dews drew quivering and chill—
For only Gossamer, my Gown—
My Tippet—only Tulle—

Continued on next page

We paused before a House that seemed
A Swelling of the Ground—
The Roof was scarcely visible—
The Cornice—in the Ground—

Since then—'tis Centuries—and yet
Feels shorter than the Day
I first surmised the Horses' Heads
Were toward Eternity—

"Questions"

"Because I could not stop for Death"

1 In the third stanza of this poem, what three stages of life are represented?

2 Most people would not choose to "stop" for Death, but no one can escape dying. What effect does Dickinson's portrayal of Death as "kindly" stopping for the speaker and taking her for an unhurried carriage ride achieve? What tone is created? What technique does she use to describe Death?

3 What do you make of the "House" the speaker pauses before in the fifth stanza; what about the way she is dressed?

4 How does structure contrast with the author's message?

"I heard a Fly buzz— when I died"

EMILY DICKINSON

I heard a Fly buzz—when I died;
The Stillness in the Room
Was like the Stillness in the Air—
Between the Heaves of Storm—

The Eyes around—had wrung them dry—
And Breaths were gathering firm
For that last Onset—when the King
Be witnessed—in the Room—

I willed my Keepsakes—Signed away
What portion of me be
Assignable—and then it was
There interposed a Fly—

With Blue—uncertain stumbling Buzz—
Between the light—and me—
And then the Windows failed—and then
I could not see to see—

"I heard a Fly buzz—when I died"

1 Look at some of the other Dickinson poems in this collection. What stylistic characteristics are similar among her poems?

2 How does the poet describe death?

3 How does Dickinson use rhyme to convey a sense of finality at the conclusion of the poem?

Holy Sonnets: X

JOHN DONNE

Death, be not proud, though some have called thee
Mighty and dreadful, for thou art not so;
For those whom thou think'st thou dost overthrow,
Die not, poor Death, nor yet canst thou kill me.
From rest and sleep, which but thy pictures be,
Much pleasure; then from thee much more must flow,
And soonest our best men with thee do go,
Rest of their bones, and soul's delivery.
Thou art slave to fate, chance, kings, and desperate men,
And dost with poison, war, and sickness dwell;
And poppy or charms can make us sleep as well
And better than thy stroke; why swell'st thou then?
One short sleep past, we wake eternally,
And death shall be no more; Death, thou shalt die.

Holy Sonnets: X

1 Contrast the way Donne personifies Death (a thing swollen with pride at his own power) with the way Dickinson personifies Death in her poem. Which poet's depiction of Death seems the more passionate? How does the tone of Donne's poem differ from the tone of Dickinson's?

2 Why is this sonnet, which does not mention God, considered one of Donne's "Holy Sonnets"? What is it, according to Donne, which "kills" Death in the end?

3 Identify some literary terms Donne uses and give examples of them. What arguments does he use to convince the reader that Death is something that people should not fear?

The Raven

EDGAR ALLAN POE

Once upon a midnight dreary, while I pondered, weak and weary,
Over many a quaint and curious volume of forgotten lore,
While I nodded, nearly napping, suddenly there came a tapping,
As of some one gently rapping, rapping at my chamber door.
" 'Tis some visitor," I muttered, "tapping at my chamber door—
      Only this, and nothing more."

Ah, distinctly I remember it was in the bleak December,
And each separate dying ember wrought its ghost upon the floor.
Eagerly I wished the morrow;—vainly I had sought to borrow
From my books surcease of sorrow—sorrow for the lost Lenore—
For the rare and radiant maiden whom the angels name Lenore—
      Nameless here for evermore.

And the silken sad uncertain rustling of each purple curtain
Thrilled me—filled me with fantastic terrors never felt before;
So that now, to still the beating of my heart, I stood repeating,
" 'Tis some visitor entreating entrance at my chamber door—
Some late visitor entreating entrance at my chamber door;—
      This it is, and nothing more."

Presently my soul grew stronger; hesitating then no longer,
"Sir," said I, "or Madam, truly your forgiveness I implore;
But the fact is I was napping, and so gently you came rapping,
And so faintly you came tapping, tapping at my chamber door,
That I scarce was sure I heard you"—here I opened wide the door;—
      Darkness there, and nothing more.

Deep into that darkness peering, long I stood there wondering, fearing,
Doubting, dreaming dreams no mortals ever dared to dream before;
But the silence was unbroken, and the stillness gave no token,
And the only word there spoken was the whispered word, "Lenore!"
This I whispered, and an echo murmured back the word, "Lenore!"—
      Merely this, and nothing more.

Back into the chamber turning, all my soul within me burning,
Soon again I heard a tapping somewhat louder than before.
"Surely," said I, "surely that is something at my window lattice:
Let me see, then, what thereat is, and this mystery explore—
Let my heart be still a moment and this mystery explore;—
      'Tis the wind and nothing more."

Open here I flung the shutter, when, with many a flirt and flutter,
In there stepped a stately raven of the saintly days of yore;
Not the least obeisance made he; not a minute stopped or stayed he;
But, with mien of lord or lady, perched above my chamber door—
Perched upon a bust of Pallas just above my chamber door—
      Perched, and sat, and nothing more.

Then this ebony bird beguiling my sad fancy into smiling,
By the grave and stern decorum of the countenance it wore.
"Though thy crest be shorn and shaven, thou," I said, "art sure no craven,
Ghastly grim and ancient raven wandering from the Nightly shore—
Tell me what thy lordly name is on the Night's Plutonian shore!"
      Quoth the Raven, "Nevermore."

Much I marvelled this ungainly fowl to hear discourse so plainly,
Though its answer little meaning—little relevancy bore;
For we cannot help agreeing that no living human being
Ever yet was blest with seeing bird above his chamber door—
Bird or beast upon the sculptured bust above his chamber door,
      With such name as "Nevermore."

Continued on next page

But the raven, sitting lonely on the placid bust, spoke only
That one word, as if his soul in that one word he did outpour.
Nothing further then he uttered—not a feather then he fluttered—
Till I scarcely more than muttered, "other friends have flown before—
On the morrow he will leave me, as my hopes have flown before."
          Then the bird said, "Nevermore."

Startled at the stillness broken by reply so aptly spoken,
"Doubtless," said I, "what it utters is its only stock and store,
Caught from some unhappy master whom unmerciful Disaster
Followed fast and followed faster till his songs one burden bore—
Till the dirges of his Hope that melancholy burden bore
          Of 'Never—nevermore'."

But the Raven still beguiling all my fancy into smiling,
Straight I wheeled a cushioned seat in front of bird, and bust and door;
Then upon the velvet sinking, I betook myself to linking
Fancy unto fancy, thinking what this ominous bird of yore—
What this grim, ungainly, ghastly, gaunt and ominous bird of yore
          Meant in croaking "Nevermore."

This I sat engaged in guessing, but no syllable expressing
To the fowl whose fiery eyes now burned into my bosom's core;
This and more I sat divining, with my head at ease reclining
On the cushion's velvet lining that the lamplight gloated o'er,
But whose velvet violet lining with the lamplight gloating o'er,
          She shall press, ah, nevermore!

Then methought the air grew denser, perfumed from an unseen censer
Swung by Seraphim whose footfalls tinkled on the tufted floor.
"Wretch," I cried, "thy God hath lent thee—by these angels he hath sent
     thee
Respite—respite and nepenthe, from thy memories of Lenore!
Quaff, oh quaff this kind nepenthe and forget this lost Lenore!"
          Quoth the Raven, "Nevermore."

"Prophet!" said I, "thing of evil!—prophet still, if bird or devil!—
Whether Tempter sent, or whether tempest tossed thee here ashore,
Desolate yet all undaunted, on this desert land enchanted—
On this home by horror haunted—tell me truly, I implore—
Is there—is there balm in Gilead?—tell me—tell me, I implore!"
        Quoth the Raven, "Nevermore."

"Prophet!" said I, "thing of evil—prophet still, if bird or devil!
By that Heaven that bends above us—by that God we both adore—
Tell this soul with sorrow laden if, within the distant Aidenn,
It shall clasp a sainted maiden whom the angels name Lenore—
Clasp a rare and radiant maiden whom the angels name Lenore."
        Quoth the Raven, "Nevermore."

"Be that word our sign in parting, bird or fiend," I shrieked, upstarting—
"Get thee back into the tempest and the Night's Plutonian shore!
Leave no black plume as a token of that lie thy soul hath spoken!
Leave my loneliness unbroken!—quit the bust above my door!
Take thy beak from out my heart, and take thy form from off my door!"
        Quoth the Raven, "Nevermore."

And the Raven, never flitting, still is sitting, still is sitting
On the pallid bust of Pallas just above my chamber door;
And his eyes have all the seeming of a demon's that is dreaming,
And the lamplight o'er him streaming throws his shadow on the floor;
And my soul from out that shadow that lies floating on the floor
        Shall be lifted—nevermore!

The Raven

① In "The Raven," what do you suppose is the significance of the repeated phrase, "Nevermore"?

② Discuss Poe's use of symbolism in the poem, particularly in the raven and the bust of Pallas Athena.

③ An allusion is a reference to another work of literature, a person, place, history, or work of art. Poe was fond of using allusions to convey a message or attach significance to ideas in his writing. One such allusion is to Pallas Athena, the goddess of wisdom. What other allusions can you find in this poem? How do allusions add to your interpretation of the poem?

④ In an essay titled "The Philosophy of Composition," Poe described the creation of "The Raven" as a calculated process, in which he first determined the effect he wanted to achieve, next his theme, and then worked backwards to accomplish his goal. You can certainly see the calculation in the resulting form of the poem—its effective rhyme, repetition, and meter. What effect do you think Poe was aiming for, and how do you see it achieved as a calculated effort?

Out, Out—

ROBERT FROST

The buzz-saw snarled and rattled in the yard
And made dust and dropped stove-length sticks of wood,
Sweet-scented stuff when the breeze drew across it.
And from there those that lifted eyes could count
Five mountain ranges one behind the other
Under the sunset far into Vermont.
And the saw snarled and rattled, snarled and rattled,
As it ran light, or had to bear a load.
And nothing happened: day was all but done.
Call it a day, I wish they might have said
To please the boy by giving him the half hour
That a boy counts so much when saved from work.
His sister stood beside them in her apron
To tell them 'Supper.' At the word, the saw,
As if to prove saws knew what supper meant,
Leaped out at the boy's hand, or seemed to leap—
He must have given the hand. However it was,
Neither refused the meeting. But the hand!
The boy's first outcry was a rueful laugh.
As he swung toward them holding up the hand
Half in appeal, but half as if to keep
The life from spilling. Then the boy saw all—
Since he was old enough to know, big boy
Doing a man's work, though a child at heart—

Continued on next page

He saw all spoiled. "Don't let him cut my hand off
The doctor, when he comes. Don't let him, sister!"
So. But the hand was gone already.
The doctor put him in the dark of ether.
He lay and puffed his lips out with his breath.
And then—the watcher at his pulse took fright.
No one believed. They listened at his heart.
Little—less—nothing!—and that ended it.
No more to build on there. And they, since they
Were not the one dead, turned to their affairs.

Questions Out, Out—

1 How does Frost's use of onomatopoeia and personification operate in the poem?

2 Given the final lines, what statement is Frost making about life and death?

3 How does the conversational tone of this poem work with form to convey Frost's message?

4 "How does Frost make the boy and the job of cutting wood with the saw similar?

Stopping By 106th & Broadway

PATRICIA BRODY

It is snowing on the synagogue across the street.
It is snowing on the mourners, swaying in the snow.
It is snowing on the deli, the sliced meat.
It is snowing on the lamppost with its other-century glow.
It is snowing on Memory, her dress, her slender feet
       jeweled in the first thin frost of snow.
It is snowing on Straus Park, the lost Titanic story:
       earth reaps the bones of Ida and Isador
       lost at sea
       (lovely and pleasant were they in their lives
       and in their death they were not divided)
       clasping—merged—in their song-filled sleep.
It is snowing on Memory, her icy feet.
It is snowing on the moth-wing scorched last July.
It is snowing on the oranges and pears left for Memory
       to wear as an offering, awkward, sweet.
It is snowing on my father.

Questions

Stopping by 106th & Broadway

1 In "For I Will Consider My Cat Jeoffrey," the author used anaphora to move the poem from one idea to the next, as Brody does in this poem. Compare the two. Which do you consider more effective, and why?

2 The final line of Brody's poem offers some insight as to her purpose in writing this poem. Why do you think it takes the entire poem to get to this point in the poem? How does time function in the poem?

3 What do you make of the line "It is snowing on Memory, her icy feet"? What is "Memory"? What comment do you suppose Brody may be making about Memory?

4 Identify, research, and explain the allusions in the poem.

Here. Now.

LAUREL K. DODGE

There is no death.
              —Jure Kaštelan*

Hours, days, years from now, I will feel
the sting: A splinter will be discovered, a sliver
of coffin, the miniature limb of a tree buried

deep beneath the skin. And I will hear
the rattle: A pebble will be found, a remembrance,
a tiny piece of the sea secreted in my pocket,

turning over and over like the tide coming in.
And I will see the flutter: A single feather will float
down from the wing of an angel, or the tail

of a peregrine. A branch will crack and fall,
a wave will curl into itself and crash upon the shore;
the shadow of a raptor will soar across

the lawn and right through me. I don't believe
in god or ghosts, hell, or heaven, yet you will be
present. Here. Now. Father, you will be.

* *Jure Kaštelan [1919-1990] was a Croatian poet.*

Questions   Here. Now.

1 What is the subject of this poem? What statement is the poet making about death?

2 Although this poem ascribes to no particular, it is written in a certain consistent pattern. Describe this consistency, and explain how you think the form of this poem serves to help Dodge make her statement. What literary terms or sound devices are used in the poem?

3 What is the author's tone in this poem? What words contribute to this effect?

Beautiful Tie

LAUREL K. DODGE

Happy Fa— oh, nevermind.
Best to let sleeping dogs die.
Lie. I swear I meant lie. It's just another
day. Like Easter or Thanksgiving.
Best not to pause and consider
death and resurrection; what
we're thankful for. Or if we're ever
forgiven. That's the beauty
of regret. I said that in my dream
as I was driving, as I was driven
through the rain. Best to let dying
dogs lie. Sleeping. It looked
as though you were sleeping.
As if you slept right through your death;
as if you'd dreamed it. Or as if I had.
What would happen if the dog
was awakened? I tried to wake you
but you never opened your eyes.
Happy Fa— oh, nevermind.
It's just another Hallmark holiday,
another card I don't have to sign
I love you, dad. Guess it's best
to let dead dads lie. If you were alive,
I would've sent you an unsigned card;
I would've bought you a beautiful tie.

Questions

Beautiful Tie

1 What is Dodge's subject matter in this poem? How is this poem different from her preceding poem, "Here. Now."?

2 Examine the effect of the plays on words Dodge uses in "Beautiful Tie" ("let sleeping dogs die"; "let dying dogs lie"; "let dead dads lie"). What do you think Dodge's purpose in using the puns was, considering the gravity of her subject matter?

3 How would you describe the form of this poem? What is the effect of the last two lines?

Not Waving but Drowning

STEVIE SMITH

Nobody heard him, the dead man,
But still he lay moaning:
I was much further out than you thought
And not waving but drowning.

Poor chap, he always loved larking
And now he's dead
It must have been too cold for him his heart gave way,
They said.

Oh, no no no, it was too cold always
(Still the dead one lay moaning)
I was much too far out all my life
And not waving but drowning.

Not Waving but Drowing

1 What is the paradox in this poem? Is the title humorous or chilling?

2 Examine Smith's poem and identify what sound devices and repetitions are in the poem. How do some of these contribute to your understanding of the poem?

3 How do the spectators misinterpret the man's life?

Do Not Go Gentle into that Good Night

DYLAN THOMAS

Do not go gentle into that good night,
Old age should burn and rave at close of day;
Rage, rage against the dying of the light.

Though wise men at their end know dark is right,
Because their words had forked no lightning they
Do not go gentle into that good night.

Good men, the last wave by, crying how bright
Their frail deeds might have danced in a green bay,
Rage, rage against the dying of the light.

Wild men who caught and sang the sun in flight,
And learn, too late, they grieved it on its way,
Do not go gentle into that good night.

Grave men, near death, who see with blinding sight
Blind eyes could blaze like meteors and be gay,
Rage, rage against the dying of the light.

And you, my father, there on the sad height,
Curse, bless, me now with your fierce tears, I pray.
Do not go gentle into that good night.
Rage, rage against the dying of the light.

Do Not Go Gentle into that Good Night

1 Who is the speaker in this poem and to whom is he speaking? What do we learn about each?

2 Thomas' poem is called a villanelle, an extremely difficult type of poetry to write due to its rigid structural guidelines. Villanelles are nineteen-lined poems that utilize only two rhyming words and contain two repeating lines of verse throughout the poem. The first five stanzas are tercets, and the last stanza is a quatrain. The rhyme scheme is ABA ABA ABA ABA ABA ABAA. Study Thomas' poem to discover the pattern in which the lines repeat themselves. What do you notice about the style of these lines?

3 This villanelle is, in essence, a battle cry against allowing death to conquer easily. Thomas identifies four categories of men and reasons why they have not truly lived, which is why they should "rage, rage against the dying of the light." Examine the second through the fifth tercets and identify these categories of men and why they have failed to live.

One Art

ELIZABETH BISHOP

The art of losing isn't hard to master;
so many things seem filled with the intent
to be lost that their loss is no disaster.

Lose something every day. Accept the fluster
of lost door keys, the hour badly spent.
The art of losing isn't hard to master.

Then practice losing farther, losing faster:
places, and names, and where it was you meant
to travel. None of these will bring disaster.

I lost my mother's watch. And look! my last, or
next-to-last, of three loved houses went.
The art of losing isn't hard to master.

I lost two cities, lovely ones. And, vaster,
some realms I owned, two rivers, a continent.
I miss them, but it wasn't a disaster.

—Even losing you (the joking voice, a gesture
I love) I shan't have lied. It's evident
the art of losing's not too hard to master
though it may look like (Write it!) like disaster.

Questions
One Art

1 Describe the tone of the poem. Does it change at all as the poem progresses?

2 Comment on the form of the poem. How does the structure help move the poem from abstracts to specifics, in terms of the author's message? What is the significance of the command in the last line?

3 Consider the various things that have been lost by the speaker. Some are easy to identify with—the lost keys, for example, or wasted time and a mother's watch. What do you think she means when she refers to "two cities, lovely ones. And, vaster / some realms I owned, two rivers, a continent"?

Glossary of Literary Terms

Alliteration – the repetition of sounds at the beginning of words.

Allusion – a reference to a person, place, poem, book, event, etc., which is not part of the story, that the author expects the reader will recognize.

Analogy – a comparison between things, people, places, etc., that are similar in order to point out the dissimilarities.

Anthropomorphism – attributing human qualities, emotions, and behavior to animals.

Apostrophe – directly addressing a person, place, thing, or abstraction, living, dead, or absent from the work

Assonance – repetition of an interior vowel sound within a short section.

Aubade – a poem that deals with morning, when lovers separate.

Ballad – a narrative poem that deals with a single incident.

Blank Verse – unrhymed lines of poetry written in iambic pentameter.

Caesura – a pause in a line of poetry, through either punctuation or meter.

Climax – the point of greatest dramatic tension or excitement in a story.

Consonance – repetition of an interior consonant sound within a short sentence.

Couplet – two successive rhyming lines of poetry, usually the same length

Direct Address – speaking directly to a person, place, thing, or abstraction, living, dead, or absent from the work [See *Apostrophe*].

Foot – a measure of length in poetry, dependent on syllables.

Free verse – poetry that has no formal rhyme or meter and depends on the rhythms of speech.

Haiku – a traditional type of Japanese poetry, consisting of seventeen syllables arranged in three unrhymed lines of five, seven, and five syllables each.

Half Rhyme – a near-rhyme; one that is approximate, not exact. Also called slant rhyme.

Hyperbole – exaggeration for emphasis; overstatement.

Iamb - the most common foot of poetry in English, made up of two syllables, the first unstressed and the second stressed.

Iambic Pentameter – a line of poetry composed of five feet of iambs; the most common form of English poetry.

Iambic Tetrameter – a line of poetry consisting of eight syllables, with the accent on the even numbered syllables.

Imagery – the use of words to evoke impressions and meanings that are more than just the basic, accepted definitions of the words themselves.

Inference - the act of drawing a conclusion that is not actually stated by the author.

Internal Rhyme – the rhyming of words within one line of poetry or one sentence of prose.

Irony – a perception of inconsistency, sometimes humorous, in which the significance and understanding of a statement or event is changed by its context.

- *Dramatic Irony* - the audience or reader knows more about a character's situation than the character does and knows that the character's understanding is incorrect.
- *Structural Irony* – the use of a naïve hero, whose incorrect perceptions differ from the reader's correct ones.
- *Verbal Irony* - a discrepancy between what is said and what is really meant; sarcasm.

Juxtaposition – the placement of two dissimilar items, people, thoughts, places, etc., next to one another to emphasize the differences or heighten the similarities.

Litotes – a conscious understatement that achieves the opposite effect of the words themselves.

Metaphor – a comparison of two things that are basically dissimilar in which one is described in terms of the other.

Meter – the emphasized pattern of repeated sounds in poetry; meter is represented by stressed and unstressed syllables.

Motif – a situation, incident, idea, or image that is repeated significantly in a literary work.

Octet – a stanza of poetry made up of eight lines; an octet is usually used as the first eight lines of a sonnet

Onomatopoeia – a word whose sound (the way it is pronounced) imitates its meaning.

Oxymoron – a term or phrase that is apparently self-contradictory.

Paradox – a statement that is self-contradictory on its surface, yet makes a point through the juxtaposition of the ideas and words within the paradox.

Parallelism – the repetition of similarly constructed phrases, clauses, or sentences within a short section.

Personification – a figure of speech in which an object, abstract idea, or animal is given human characteristics.

Pun - an expression that achieves emphasis or humor by utilizing two distinctly different meanings for the same word or two similar sounding words.

Quatrain – a four-lined stanza of poetry.

Rhyme Scheme – an alphabetical representation of the way a poem rhymes, constructed by assigning each line a letter.

Sarcasm – the use of harsh words to deride and criticize. Sometimes, sarcasm is apparent only by the way something is said rather than the actual words that are used; other times the sarcasm is obvious.

Sestet – a stanza of poetry made up of six lines; a sestet is usually used as the last six lines of a sonnet.

Setting – when and where the short story, play, poem, or novel takes place.

Simile – a comparison between two different things using either *like* or *as*.

Sonnet – a fourteen line poem written in iambic pentameter and having a standard rhyme scheme.

Stanza – the grouping of lines in a poem.

Stream of Consciousness – the continuous flow of sense perceptions, thoughts, feelings, and memories in the human mind; a literary method of representing such a blending of mental processes in fictional characters.

Symbol – an object, person, or place that has a meaning in itself and that also stands for something larger than itself, usually an idea or concept; some concrete thing which represents an abstraction.

Synecdoche – using a part of something to stand for the entire thing.

Tercet – a grouping of three consecutive lines of poetry that may or may not rhyme.

Tetrameter – a verse in a poem consisting of four metric feet.

Theme – the central or dominant idea behind the work of literature; the most important aspect that emerges from how the subject is treated.

Tone – the atmosphere in a literary work or the attitude the author puts in a literary work. *Trimeter* – a line of a poem that contains three metric feet.

Verisimilitude – the use of realistic elements to make literature appear truthful or accurate.